A
SCATTERING
OF CATS

Sandra Bozarth

Illustrated by
Alice Horst

LOST〰
COAST
PRESS
Fort Bragg
California

LOST COAST PRESS
155 Cypress Street
Fort Bragg, CA 95437
1-800-773-7782
www.cypresshouse.com

Cover art and illustrations: Alice Horst, "Alz," 1996
Cover design: Michael Brechner / Cypress House

Frontispiece: facsimile of linoleum block print,
Virgil Bozarth, 1938, by CGA (Concord Graphic Arts), 1996

Excerpt from "The Ghost Continent" in *The Unexpected Universe*, copyright © 1969 by Loren Eiseley, reprinted by permission of Harcourt, Inc.

Library of Congress Cataloging-in Publication Data
Bozarth, Sandra, 1934-
  A scattering of cats / Sandra Bozarth.
    p. cm.
  ISBN 1-882897-66-8
    1. Cats--Anecdotes. 2. Cat owners--Anecdotes.
3. Bozarth, Sandra, 1934- I. Title.
  SF445.5 B68 2002
  636.8'0887--dc21   2001037705

⊗The paper used in this publication meets the minimum requirements of the American National Standard for Information Sciences—Permanence of Paper for Printed Library Materials, ANSI Z39.48-1984

2 4 6 8 9 7 5 3

To each,

MY GRATITUDE:

Alice Horst, "Alz," for decades of friendship, for
criticisms of the drafts, for the drawings
that grace these pages.

Ginger Ogden and John Willson for being my
neighbors, and because Mom Cat started it all.

The Martinez Animal Hospital:
Carl E. Monser, D.V.M., for the veterinary critique.
For background details:
Carol Coleman, R.V.T.
Elana Easter
Stacy J. Enke, D.V.M.
Bev Hanson

Diablo View Veterinary Medical Hospital:
Carol Beebee

Hilda Johnston, for her unbiased
analysis of parts of the manuscript.

And memory joggers:
Charlene Perry
Terri Telfer-Uhlir
Jim Whisenand

Thank you!
Sandra Bozarth

CONTENTS

In Memory
of my parents

MICKEY AND VIRGIL

whose ashes face
the sunrises over
Mount Diablo

1996

The magic that gleams an instant between
Argos and Odysseus is both the recognition
of diversity and the need for affection
across the illusions of form.

— Loren Eiseley, *The Unexpected Universe*

1

OPALS

Mo loses me in the house and goes about calling, a pure sound, plaintive and anxious: *Where are you?* "Here, Mo. I'm down here, in my office." His gray and white head appears at the top of the basement stairs. Down he comes, thump "Murr," thump "Murr," all the way to the bottom, expressing — something — relief, perhaps. He jumps onto the swivel chair to the right of my wooden desk-table, settles into a ball and murmurs himself to sleep. I look at him and wonder what world spins away its time in his head.

As I watch him, I see other times. He finds me outside and leans his shoulder into me, giving me his balance to keep for him. He finds me at the kitchen table, hops to my lap with a small cry, and molds himself to my shape. I see then into the crystal of his eyes. His white-furred throat sinks into my hands, and his purr vibrates up through my palms. We drift in a moment out of time.

When I was a child, my mother had an opal ring, the stone oval, a light clear blue swirled with milky white. Somewhere in its depths were glints of liquid yellow and of pink sparks. I liked to bring the stone slowly right up to my eye, losing myself in the soft, cool fire of a different dimension. What universe was in there? Looking into the jewel eyes of the cats is like looking into that opal. What is it to have a feline's brain? What goes on in the mind behind that eye? Something does, I think, something that is not all raw instinct.

That something has surprised me with insights and unanswered questions all through the years in this white frame house where I have grown up. Like my mother's ring, each of the many cats has contained a marvel and a mystery.

Here is a scattering of those opals. Some are etched by the years, but their essence shines like the light in Mo's green eyes.

1937 ~ 1939

2

SNAPSHOT

It is black and white, about two inches by three, with a gently scalloped white edging. Through this border runs a fine, black line which frames and gives significance to the world it contains. Some quality of the little photo, perhaps the dignity of its understatement, tugs me through its rectangle and back in time onto the steep, California hillside within. I lean forward to keep my balance on the gradient; I feel my throat stretch as I lift my head to see the tall, white house rising out of the hill near the top.

Martinez was a small town, and in the 1930s few human structures interrupted the sweep of the encircling hills. Toward the western ridge, they rose huge and steep and domed, one tier above another, daubed with chaparral, an occasional bay tree, and cupolas of buckeyes which reached nearly to the ground. The wild grasses were a soft, bright green in the winter and spring, a dusty gold over gray-brown earth, baked and cracked, in the summer. Always there were the dark blue-green, rough clumps of the oaks.

Just a seedling then, one of the live oaks was growing west of center on the north-facing terrace of that white house in the snapshot. The house was new. It was the first one way up there on Panoramic Drive, and it stood devoid of landscaping on the upper third of its quarter acre. Below the terrace was the lower lot, and from just inside its white paddock fence at the bottom, one could glimpse a stucco corner of house number two to the east.

Where then, with so few people, did all the cats come from? My parents and I would see them as they broke cover and dashed across an open spot. Always they were gray and thin. There was a wildness about them that said they had never known a hearth or a human touch. If a door opened or a voice called out, they would melt instantly into the brush.

One spring afternoon my father was down on the lower lot where he intended to plant a few toyons. When he stepped toward a thick row of volunteer geraniums, red against a stretch of the paddock fence, there was a sudden rustling flurry from the base of the heavy growth. Spitting and hissing, a small, gray animal sprang out, wrapped itself around my father's right leg, and sank razor claws through the twill fabric into his flesh. Dad yelled and stamped, shook his leg and swiped at the creature, but the cat hung on with frightening purpose. Dad dared not reach for its nape. He grabbed his spade, scraped at his leg, and the cat dropped to the ground. It retreated into the undergrowth, still snarling.

Dad stood, breathing a little hard, adrenalin still pumping but not covering the burn of the ragged scratches. He went back up and over to where the attack had begun. He listened, then knelt, parting the grasses and revealing a little clearing under the geraniums. There was the nest. Four new kittens clung to one another, ears tight on the wobbling heads, eyes just furry slits. One of them began to mew.

What would become of the kittens and of their brave, wild mother? We would never be able to tame her, and for whatever reason — probably because they were so very young and the mother would hide them again anyway — we did not try to adopt the babies.

The next day the kittens were gone. We did not see them or the mother again.

But the house was new, and there would be many cats.

3

MORNING

Would it happen today? Would the gray kitty have her babies today? The new morning's light reached into me, and the question fluttered up from my stomach as my eyes flew open. Was I old enough to watch the kittens come out of their mother? It was almost spring, but I would not be six until November. That was a very long time away. I gazed out the dormer window — how high up my room was — and watched the sunlight flow down the trees on this side of the woods. Enchanted woods. They were higher even than our house, which was enchanted, too. I hugged Limpy cat, and looked into the button eyes on his plaid face. From somewhere out in the thin air came a three-note bird song on a down-sliding scale. It came every morning, but I never saw the bird. The slow, pure sounds, repeated over and over, always spilled out so lonely and sad and beautiful that my throat knotted up. But only for a moment. The blue-skied mornings brought fun things, too. Like the gray kitty with her big, big tummy. I plopped Limpy on the pillow, jumped up, and dressed myself. It could happen today!

I remembered to be careful going down the thirteen oak steps to the living room — too many times I had rolled and bumped on the hard wood all the way to the bottom — and then I ran. I heard Mother in the kitchen; dishes clinked and the refrigerator snicked shut. I reached up to pull open the front door, made the one step down to the porch, and stopped. Not even my impatience could lessen the impact on me of the newness, the beginning, called "morning." It was early, maybe seven, and the slanting light was gilding the pink bricks of the walk on my right, the three steps up to the porch, and the door which I turned to close. It was a tongue-in-groove Dutch door with a six pane window set in the upper half. Daddy had mixed his own paint colors; the door gleamed softly in a green like the spruce trees at Christmas. I reached up for the dull brass handle, and felt the curving patterns like flower stems in the long part under the thumb rest. There was a whole world right here on the bricks of the porch.

But I had to hurry, before breakfast would happen. I turned and skipped across the short end of the porch and down a step to peer in suspense through the garage window. At the front a cardboard box had been set a little way off the concrete floor. It was lined with newspaper and faded blue toweling. My breath caught; she was there!

I opened the door and went down into the garage and carefully over to the box. The gray cat lay there, her middle huge with kittens, and blinked at me unconcernedly. Her labor had already begun. Without touching her I settled down to watch.

Soon the spasms came rippling over her belly. The muscles tightened and defined the shapes moving inside. She raised her head and looked toward her rear; soon the first kitten was nearly out, and then it was out. She bent over herself to tear off the whitish membrane and bite through the little cord. I had never seen this before, and I felt all excited and grown up. The mother licked the kitten briskly, the pink sickle of her tongue shoving him about and tumbling him over. How could the tiny paws be so perfect? And, look! Claws — teensy, curving slivers! My face was practically in the box. More contractions interrupted the mother, and before long there was a second kitten and more licking. I got up and ran into the house and into the kitchen to make my important announcement. My parents were all wide eyes and open mouths. We sat down to breakfast and talked about cats and kittens.

I could not long sit still, however, and shortly I was back in the garage. There was a third kitten! The mother was resting. All three babies were suckling, little arms crooked at the elbows, miniature, needle-tipped paws pushing rhythmically — first one and then the other — against the sides of the swollen udders. Entranced, I settled in on the concrete, ready to spend the morning there. I watched the mother's breathing lift and lower the kittens in a gently rocking motion. Her belly still looked big, and a short vigil rewarded me with two more babies. The fifth one had a brownish undercoat topped with black up-and-down stripes. The white feet showed mostly clean, pink skin, and the little nose was all pink, too. I liked this one the best. But, oh my, five kittens! I ran inside and reported. "Goodness!" said my mother with appropriate surprise and perhaps just a bit of consternation. "Five kittens! We'll come out soon and see them."

But when I announced the sixth one, and after a while the eighth one, Mother and Daddy turned skeptical. "Are you sure, Sandra girl?" they asked, and I was affronted. I was not fibbing, and at five and one-half years of age I certainly could count to eight! So, we all went out to see the kittens, and sure enough eight there were. The mother cat was stretched out, tired but content, and everybody had found a fountain. I stayed on my knees by the box a long time. I watched and watched, and tried to absorb this miracle and not burst with wanting to jump up and down. This was an exciting, sunny morning, and in the cool, secure garage new life had begun. The world was perfect.

As the days passed, my favorite kitten became "Pinky." Another was "Brownie," and the fuzzy, gray one was "Agamemnon," a name from a small, cherished storybook with photographs of kittens all dressed up in short pants and little straw hats. I could pet the babies now, could pick them up to hold them close to my face and feel their tiny, squirming softness. They had a pleasant smell of moist, very clean fur.

1941

4

COMFORT

Changes new and wonderful to me marked the passing of the months following the kittens' birth. I watched small, round heads develop larger eyes and longer noses. Ear nubs grew into soft triangles that swiveled to catch sounds and to express anger, eager interest, or indecision. Fat milk bellies slimmed down. Stubby legs, once so hesitant and shaky, became longer and deft.

Always an outside cat, the mother cared well for her kittens. Through her they learned to be cautious, and to hunt with patience and precision the abundant moles, gophers, and field mice which shared our hill. But some things were beyond her to teach or to prevent. In the early fall, Agamemnon died of distemper. I did not understand. He had been so pretty with his tabby stripes on light gray. How could a creature so sweet and soft get sick? How could he die?

Even in the car the next day I thought about this. "Dying" meant that Agamemnon was gone. He could never come back. He could never see or feel. I stared out the window and watched the last of the houses run back from the car along the narrow road. The land opened and flattened into Alhambra Valley. Rows and rows of pear trees marched down straight lines to become far-away dots. Through the open car windows came the perfume of the fruit ripening on the trees. We turned right onto a dirt lane to the Swett Ranch, and inched along so as to not raise the brown dust. Trees and trees and trees! This, too, was a world. Drooping branches were propped up with poles and boards. Ladders leaned on trunks. Pears hung down, rosy yellow and heavy, among the green leaves. Trays of apples, apricots, plums, and pears stood drying in the sun. Bees hummed. Flies buzzed. The sunny air smelled like our kitchen when mother cooked jam. The people on the ladders and in the sheds had black, straight hair, almond-shaped eyes, and names like "Yamamoto" and "Ueda," that sounded like notes from a flute. Their smiles stretched up and wrinkled their faces and showed their teeth. They bowed when they spoke to us, and their bows were like birds dipping to drink. Even their voices were the voices of small birds. One couple, the Fukuchis, was taller than many, and spoke more English. They were our friends, and at Christmas time they always came to our house with trays of dried fruit wrapped in cellophane.

But this year on December 7 the radio spoke of nothing

but "Pearl Harbor." At lunch in the kitchen we listened to reports, and I listened to Mother and Daddy. Later I stood with my back against the refrigerator and tried to understand how people had died on Pearl Harbor, and what "death" really meant. I guessed that, like Agamemnon, it meant those people could never come back. Someone dead could not bite a red apple, hear it pop, or catch its juice on his tongue. He could not watch a blue jay swap ends on a branch, or feel the warm softness of a stripy kitten with white paws. "Death" must mean "not being any more." So the other people, the ones at the Swett Ranch, the people who smiled and bowed, were our enemies now. They could make us not be. I did not like them anymore.

This time when the Fukuchis came, I ran to hide in the kitchen. I could see them standing in the living room, Mr. Fukuchi looking at the floor with his mouth pulled down, Mrs. Fukuchi bowing and crying and holding her hand to her mouth. I saw it then, the tray of dried fruit. Mother brought it to the kitchen and stood staring at it. Her big eyes were red and wet. I scowled at the tray, sure that if we ate the beautiful fruit we would not be anymore. Mother blew her nose and returned to our guests, and I tried to stuff the fruit into the waste can under the sink.

The next time we went to the Swett Ranch, I did not see any of the people with the straight black hair.

Six months later Brownie cat disappeared and never returned. Another death? We missed his studious look, his black-rimmed glasses and the three black frown marks between his eyes. Pinky, however, stayed healthy and playful, and entered his second year looking handsome with his black stripes over the tan base coat. Pink feet were now white to complement his snowy vest, and the pink nose leather had darkened to a dull copper. As the favorite, he was allowed to spend parts of his days inside, and he was my special companion. I missed him even if we were gone only a day; from the rear seat of the car I would sing about him all the way home. Back at last I would find him, take a front paw in each hand, and dance him around in a circle.

Pinky was still two years old the night I woke with an earache. It smothered me in a cocoon of agony. Daylight arrived, and Pinky was left outside. I stayed curled in bed, rigid and whining through clenched teeth as hour after hour crept past. The doctor came that day or the next, and then one or two times a week for many weeks. Both my ears were infected. Mother fixed my favorite soups, and looked at me as she plumped my pillows, and brought me my Limpy cat or my Snuffy dog. But the pain jerked my hand as I reached for my spoon, and it turned my beloved animals into dull lumps of cloth. Dad sat on my bed and told me stories, and rocked me when I shrank into myself with the hurt.

There were so terribly many of the big, chalky, sulfa pills to take, and ear drops to be endured every few hours. The pills would dissolve into powdery grit with the first touch of moisture, and my throat learned to close on them against my will. I gagged on their sour bitterness, and swallowing them at all became a dreaded ordeal.

The ear drops were heated; to me they felt molten and seemed to sear right to the core of my head. Both ears were stuffed with cotton. I was isolated by a world gone remote and muffled. Pinky had not been in for a long time, and I was lonely.

My daytimes now were spent on the big couch in the living room, where the unvarnished pine walls were light and yet cozy. From there, swathed in an afghan, my head on my medicine-stained pillow, I could see out the mullioned panes of the bay window. It was a huge window, running from floor to ceiling and from side to side of most of the room's north wall. I could look down onto the steep, lower lot with its paddock fencing. Below the fence I could glimpse the curve of the narrow road. Below it, the wooded hill sloped its way past an occasional house and on down to the town below. I could see the straits, the ferry as it crossed between Martinez and Benicia, and the bare hills beyond. Mother would turn the volume high on the radio — I could feel the vibrations up through the couch — for even without the cotton in my ears sounds were ghostly and far away. I floated unconnected to my world. I grasped at what I could see around me.

Our house had flowered from a mix of my father's memories and imaginings: the hardwood floors in the Iowa farmhouse of his childhood; the tall, spare, houses of Maine's craggy coast; rough, solid wooden beams. He had gathered items, from generations ago or from other lands, of brass and copper. There were glass goblets and flasks in liquid greens, cobalt blue, bright red, all radiant in the morning light. My favorite was a glass jug with a handle. It was brown, brown like the tobacco in the middle of Daddy's cigarettes, and on both sides it had long curls of grape stems and bunches of grapes, all bumpy. I liked their cool roundness against my fingers. When the sun came up through the big dining room windows, the brown jug turned gold and looked liquid, and the liquid filled the grapes and spilled into the room. I could see the jug from where I lay on the couch.

Along the tops of the windows ran the curtains. They were cream colored, edged in brick-red piping, and had men in red coats on brown horses. Mother had made those curtains. She had made all our curtains and the slip covers for many of our chairs and cushions. When the upstairs was being finished, she had worked night after night and all day long Saturdays and Sundays alongside my driven and not always patient father. Until nine, ten, or eleven at night they had hammered and sawed and sanded by the glare of naked bulbs at the ends of long, green, double cords. Before bedtime I had played among the uprights of what was becoming the big bedroom across the hall from my own smaller, west-facing room.

Remembering things and looking around helped, but the earaches were treacherous. One day I huddled with one hand clamped over my mouth, the other clawing my ear while shrieks tore out of me on their own. Through tears I glanced at the front door, half afraid someone might be staring in. Someone was. It was Pinky's face I saw, his mouth wide open with what must have been screams to match my own. He had leapt all that way from the porch to the windows in the top half of the door, where he was scrabbling to get a hold on the narrow mullions. His head disappeared as he fell back to the bricks, but in a moment he was up there again, a wild look in his eyes. From the kitchen mother heard what I could not — Pinky's yowls and the thumping and frenzied clawing. She ran and opened the door just as he was sliding off again, and in he darted. Tail up he trotted to where I was on the couch. He hopped up just as if door-leaping and yowling and being on the sofa were his daily routine. He looked at me and talked to me, and I looked at him and told him I loved him, and how wonderful it was to see him. I felt him purr as he rubbed against my side. I propped myself on one elbow, encircled him with my free arm, and he lay down next to me. The couch had always been strictly forbidden to him, and I wondered if Mother and Daddy would let him stay. I looked up. They glanced at each other. They looked down at me, at Pinky curled in the circle of my arm. They smiled, and I sank back against my pillows with my cat beside me.

So it began. When my pain was too much, Pinky would leap to that window and yowl, and Mother or Daddy would run to open the door. On the couch my cat and I would have long, cuddly visits full of his purrs and my smiles, and the awful pain would seem less. When at last after many weeks I no longer screamed, Pinky no longer jumped to the window.

My father, taking much care and a great deal of time, eventually succeeded in sanding away most of the claw damage from the door, and repainted it.

1943 ~ Spring 1946

5

J ~ CURVE

Those earaches are well over fifty years ago. Their legacy, beginning in young middle age, is a pair of hearing aids which continues to be a necessity all my waking hours. Time has brought other changes, too. Mother is gone, and my father died after six years of being unable even to raise himself to a sitting position or to turn over in bed. The house is mine now. It is an often distressing mixture of blessings and lonely burdens, of constant hard work, of memories and ghosts which overwhelm me but which are to be honored even as I strive to move on. It is a place where birds sing, cats sleep curled in the morning's warmth, and the dark foliage of the live oaks unfolds before me for a long, tranquil distance. In the cathedral silences of the upper air big red-tails and sooty turkey buzzards hover in slow spirals.

From down by the waterfront there drifts the occasional whistle and rumble of a train. This is my home.

Just now it is early morning. I have made my bed and come downstairs to find the sun sliding up from behind Mount Diablo and streaming its yellow light through my wide, kitchen windows. Mo — his plush gray and white coat still warm from sleep — is having his morning crunchies inside by the back door. I find I am out of fresh fruit, so from the basement supply cabinets I bring up a can of apricots. I am not fond of canned foods, and I have not made use of my backup rations since before Mo came to live with me. The moment I squeeze the handle of the can opener and its teeth crunch through the metal, Mo is all eager alertness. Forgotten is the bowl on the floor. He watches my hands and meows — such urgent questions — as I grind the opener around the rim of the can. So! He knows what a can opener is for. My shock turns to chagrin. Whose cat do I have? It is not the first time I ask myself this, but I cannot deny now that he has had a home, that he has been fed canned food. Was he dumped? Did he simply wander off? Why? Why, when our paths first met, had he been so obviously without a home? I stare unseeing out the window over the sink. Mo, my stray. There had always been strays.

And always they came to our house. Among the scatter of homes that had risen on the hill in the first few years, ours was the only one without a dog. Our lower lot with its growing miniature jungle of toyons, pyracantha, wild blackberry, cotoneaster, and elderberry made a refuge for feral cats, and sheltered their fretful, edgy existence. At first it was not a problem. Pinky was our only pet, and there were only two semi-wild cats that came at meal times. We would feed them out on the back terrace a few yards from the back door. They came in a crouch, looking around with wide eyes, placing each foot as if in a slow ballet. We would stand as still as posts while they snatched ravenous bites of table scraps. If we spoke even in a whisper, or started to kneel toward them, they were gone in a frantic scramble, only to return at the next feeding.

Over time others began to appear, really wild ones. They were thin, and had about them the abruptness and furtiveness of animals which know themselves as both predator and prey. We began to be caught in a cycle which we did not know how to break. In a few months there were about six of the creatures who cowered around the dishes, and meal times became events. We would watch the cats come to snarl and jostle around the food and then to flee back into the grasses and undergrowth of the hill. As the days merged into weeks and the weeks into more months, the six or seven cats became ten. My father laughed at the absurdity of it all, and muttered about when — and how — it would end.

One day when I was nine my parents' friend Mr. Christian was at our house for dinner. Pinky had joined us in the dining room and was sitting at a respectful but hopeful distance, waiting for someone to carry a plate to the kitchen. Mr. Christian eyed him and remarked, "What a handsome fellow. Is this Pinky?"

I sat up straighter and nodded. "Yes."

"An 'only' cat?"

"Well," I began, not knowing quite how to answer.

My glance slid to my father, and I knew that only Mother and I would see the anger darkening his brown eyes. "He's the only one that's really ours."

Mr. Christian grinned at Daddy. "You're granting sanctuary to errant felines?"

Mother rose quickly from the table, saying, "I'm going to feed them now, Russ. Come watch." Pinky led the way through the kitchen and went on outside with Mother. The screen door fell shut with a little bang, and our guest peered out in polite interest, but there was nothing to see. Mother stooped to put food down for Pinky a little off to one side, and stood again. Everything was quiet. There was no sign of any other animal anywhere. Then she began scraping the plates, and cats erupted from all around up and down the hill, leaving a shivering wake among the various bushes and plants. Mr. Christian's mouth opened first in disbelief and then laughter as a living circle formed at a short distance around Mother. She stayed unmoving, and he counted tails. There were thirteen.

It had gone too far. Dad discarded the options of just not feeding them, of setting traps, of using poisons. Everything seemed ineffective, unsure, threatening to Pinky or wildlife, or cruel. But when the number climbed to fifteen, he set his jaw and made a decision. As a young man in basic training for the army in World War I, he had become an excellent marksman. There had never been guns in our house, but there was another big war now, and Alhambra High School, where Dad was principal, had a cadet corps. One Friday Dad spoke with the teacher in charge, checked out a rifle, and somewhere he obtained some shells. That afternoon and the next day there was a sullen tension in the house. Twice Dad went out, waited, and sighted along the length of the rifle's cold steel. Twice he withdrew in revulsion. But the next afternoon he gained control of himself. I was not around when it happened. It was years later when he told me about it. He shot the first one, a perfect shot between the eyes. The little creature died instantly, and just as instantly the others vanished. Dad knelt down by the warm, small body, and he felt sick and stymied. There were no more shootings. Slowly at first, even as they had come, the cats disappeared. After a few weeks we had only our Pinky again.

My hand has settled back on the partly opened can of apricots, and I am aware that Mo, my stray, is tapping my leg with a white paw. *Isn't there anything in there for me?* I look down and feel so glad for him, but also guilty. In whose kitchen did he used to sit? I pour out a few more of his crunchies and top them with bits of a corn chip, a favorite treat.

6

NOBLESSE
OBLIGE

Almost four years had passed since the Fukuchis' tearful good-bye. Across the ocean cities were still in flames. Great masses of people were dying unspeakable deaths, and I learned the word, "extermination." I was growing up with the names, "Churchill," "Roosevelt," "Hitler." On the marble-topped table by the living room rocker was a magazine whose cover was a photograph of a little boy my age in a beret and knee pants. His hands were up. His face was twisted in terror as a heavy-coated soldier poked a gun in his back. My age. If I lived there, ... I had nightmares in which men in brown uniforms and wide black belts prodded me along in a wobbly mass of people with eyes and mouths like white eggs. I hid in yellow rooms that tumbled out of nowhere, but the men always found me and kicked me back into the tangled forest of gray legs. It was my turn to be shot. The men lifted their guns. I woke up.

Far over the western end of the Carquinez Straits we could sometimes see barrage balloons. Martinez had an air raid siren, terrifying in its significance and its loudness. There were nighttime blackout drills in which Mother and Daddy and I sat and whispered in the black air of the living room, and peered down into the flat darkness that had swallowed the town.

But certainly the war was far from my child's mind the shimmery spring morning of my discovery. I was outside at the back of the house when suddenly up on the bank a place in the ivy shuddered, then was still. Something was there. Another shudder, and in an easy arc a cat lifted out of cover. In mid leap she spotted me, twisted to one side, and bounded away with a frightened glance over her shoulder. She was Pinky's mate, a big gray with an appealing kind of wistful expression. She would have liked to be tame, to live here, but she could not bring herself to let us get too close, could not even long endure our softly spoken assurances. I stayed where I was, unmoving, saying nothing, but she disappeared beyond our pergola toward the lee of the west hill, where the woods began.

I was turning away when I heard a faint cry that could only mean a forlorn kitten. So that was where she had them! Excited, I went up through the gate and carefully, quietly, over to that spot in the ivy. I squatted, parted the heavy leaves, groped, and then I saw them. Three kittens, maybe two or three weeks old. They tried to scramble away, but they were too young and wobbly; their legs tangled among the stout ivy tendrils, and they sprawled helplessly under the leaves. They would not go far in this dense growth that towered above them. One little fellow was a fluff of bluish gray, one was a small copy of Pinky, and the third — with its silvery gray undercoat topped with black bars — reminded me of Agamemnon. I knew better than to touch them, and retreated.

We had known that the gray was pregnant, and that Pinky was the father. They were friends, and wherever Pinky was on the back or lower terrace we often saw her, too. We had watched as her belly swelled, became heavy, and pulled at her back such that when she sank down and moved quickly she seemed without legs. Then she had vanished for a few days. When next we glimpsed her she was slim again, but we neither saw nor heard any kittens. And now here they were. I told Mother and Daddy, and as the days passed we observed from our back door as the gray came and went. She began bringing a mouse or a gopher to the nest, and we would watch the ivy twitch as it closed first over her back, then over her tail. Pinky watched, too, but he did not intrude.

Then one day Dad found the mother cat dead on the edge of the road below the lower lot. Perhaps a car, perhaps a poison — we could not know. What now of the kittens? Like their mother they were wild. They were too young to hunt but old enough to scrabble away at our approach. We tried to bring them food, to leave water, but they hissed and jumped back. We succeeded only in forcing them, frantic and innocent, toward the upper road. So, we left them alone. They had each other and at least some shelter. When they felt thirst, perhaps their survival instinct would lead them to the water bowl at the base of the low, stone wall near the kitchen door.

But by mid morning the next day the kittens were mewling, and their high, frightened voices pierced us with guilt. Pinky heard them, also. He had been sitting, listening. Suddenly he stood, hopped up the stone wall and ducked under the paddock fence, advancing on the sound of the mewing. He was cautious. I followed and held my breath. Would he attack the kittens? Would he consider them prey? He stepped gingerly into the nest, and was greeted by eager cries and thrusting muzzles. He was unsure, sniffing at the babies only to jerk his head back as if stung, then reaching with a tentative paw to give one or the other little head a flurry of taps. The youngsters were not put off, however, and they crowded him, wanting to be fed. One pushed under him and tried to nurse, and with that Pinky leaped away.

But they intrigued him, and we saw him make another visit in the afternoon. The next day he went off to the woods, a favorite hunting ground. An hour or so later I heard him as he returned, head high with his catch. He was calling, warbling over and over from deep inside his throat and ending each time on a rising note. The sounds came muffled around a mouse, but they were big sounds and carried far and filled the still air. I watched him come, as I had done many times, and knew he would deposit his trophy at my feet. But this time it was not for me. He jumped onto the stone wall and made a wavering path up through the ivy to the kittens.

I felt my eyes stretch at what I saw next. Pinky settled

among the ravenous youngsters, shredded his prey, and watched the kittens bumble about snatching bites of meat and making brave little warning growls at one another. When they finished, Pinky ate what remained, and then sat contemplating his charges. The little fellow who resembled Pinky was looking up at him, his gaze a bit unfocused out of eyes that still retained a trace of their babyhood blueness. Pinky lowered his muzzle, they sniffed each other, and Pinky began a thorough wash of the little one's face. The kitten with the silvery gray fur and black stripes — the one which made me think so much of Agamemnon — had started to wander off. Pinky pinned him down and, having finished with the first baby, began washing this one. The kitten wriggled and struggled, received a disciplinary bite, and rolled over on his back. I smiled; this was a pretty youngster, and we should name him. I considered calling him "Agamemnon." But perhaps that was not a good idea. The first Agamemnon had died so young, and I did not want the same thing to happen to this one.

Pinky had had enough, and he came back through the ivy and down off the stone wall. We went into the kitchen. There would be a saucer of milk for him, and I could smell the warm sugar cookies that mother had taken from the oven.

7

TOO SOON

That springtime, so bright green and as cool as mint, evolved into summer's dryness and heat. The wild oats — they were everywhere on the swelling hills — turned first to green-gold, their cloven heads heavy with the furred, ripening grain. Then all at once their stalks were thin and dry and a brownish yellow. The empty oat heads were just papery husks, their substance gone. The earth, too, seemed to shrink in on itself, withering. Brown dust began to seep into cracks and little fissures. How did this always happen such that I became aware of all that bursting first fullness of life only after it was gone? Something important missed, a time slipped away and not retrievable. I was annoyed with myself.

I was not yet one, however, to fully articulate such thoughts or to dwell on them. Besides, it did not matter then. The shucked grain simply was beginning another exciting arc of the cycle. Summers had a strength and beauty and a time of their own. I was at the beginning of a school vacation which stretched ahead open and free, full of wonderful prospects including that of watching Pinky raise his kittens.

He spent hours with them every day. He watched their mock, stiff-legged fights, and sometimes he joined them. He washed their faces, which they held up to him. He licked down the lengths of their rounded backs and pudgy tummies, and pinned them down to clean their little rears. When they attempted to nurse, his paw sent them rolling and sprawling, until at last they gave it up. When they were asleep, he would go hunting. He never failed to bring a mouse or a mole or a gopher, and he began to supervise as they finished the kills.

Through Pinky the kittens began to lose their wildness. At last they hurried toward us, eager for attention and a gentle scratching along their heads and backs. They had names now, too, and the personal significance that names impart: they were "Junior," "Smoky," and the one who looked like Agamemnon was "Timmy." He was an independent little fellow, and I wondered if he would grow to be a wanderer.

Our cats would go away for two or three days, sort of camping out, and we took both their absences and their returns for what they were — mundane and unremarkable. So, when the kittens had become more self sufficient, and Pinky went off one morning near the end of summer and did not return that evening nor the next day or night, we were not particularly concerned. By the fifth day, however, we were anxious. The youngsters were fine — we had begun feeding them near the back door — but it was unlike Pinky to be gone this long.

Then one morning he reappeared in the pergola. I ran toward him, then stopped and gaped. His always shiny coat was dull and rough, the sparkling snow of his vest matted and smudged. The milky third eyelids had slid across all but glazed slits of his eyes. He breathed heavily. "Pinky!" He moved toward me, limping; a front paw was badly swollen and had small, pink-rimmed puncture wounds.

For days we kept him inside, encouraging him to eat, to drink, and waiting for his fever to break. One busy afternoon in the kitchen Mother stepped on his swollen foot; it burst with a "pop" and spurted pus and blood onto the floor and the wall. Our nostrils closed against the stench. After that he seemed better, and he spent more time outdoors in his favorite sunny spot, at the base of the strawberry tree.

Then it happened all over again with the other front paw. I begged to take him to a veterinarian, but I knew what the answer would be. Dad came from a rural background where the pet dogs and cats were loved and well cared for, but the expense of a veterinarian could be tolerated only for the commercial dairy cattle and for the horses who had to help plow the land, harvest the crops, and haul a buggy or a produce wagon to town miles away. So, the pattern had been set. And now we had a big house built with maximum work and minimum funds just on the tail of the Great Depression. The monthly payments had to be met. Veterinarians were an expensive luxury not to be considered. Besides, there was no veterinarian in Martinez. Like the pets on the long ago Iowa farm, Pinky would have to fare as best he could.

I tried to clean his vest for him and to comb his dry fur, but he drew away from me. There was a detached, inwardly focusing quality about him, and he moved tiredly away to crawl under a bush. In a few days, he disappeared. Mother told me he had probably gone away to die. She said I must not hope too much to see him again, that I must be brave. I nodded and turned away, knowing that trying to speak would only release a burst of noisy, humiliating sobs.

Days later Pinky did return, but the sight of him hit me in the stomach like one of the kickballs at school. He tottered and staggered. His breathing was a labored effort. The tip of his tongue protruded from between clenched teeth. Both hind paws were hugely swollen, and there were those same puncture marks slickly rimmed in a hairless, repulsive pink. *What awful thing was out there? Why did he keep going back into it? Stupid! Stupid, dumb cat!*

This time I did not hold back my tears. When Mother saw him, a look of shock pinched her face, and for a moment she did not speak. But soon she and Daddy were searching through the telephone book for a veterinarian. They found one somewhere, and we were on our way down the hill. Sitting there between my parents in the car, Pinky quiet in my arms, I tried to sort out my confusion of feelings. Urgency: it seemed as if time held back the car and that, as in a nightmare, we were barely moving. But inside the car time was rushing through Pinky, and I was afraid he would die before we arrived. How could time be both ways at once? Hope: the doctor would know what to do, wouldn't he? Guilt and anxiety: Daddy's silence, I knew, was a lid tightly screwed down on annoyance over the money we would have to spend and on his concern for my cat.

Suddenly we were on our way home again. That veterinarian was not a nice man. He didn't care. He didn't even think Pinky was very sick. But he was. I knew he was. Back home the three of us fixed a cardboard box with newspaper and soft, old towels. We placed Pinky in it on the bricks of the back terrace where there was part sun and part shade. Mother and Daddy went back to their chores, but I could not pull myself away. I squatted there by the box and looked down in despair at the inert shape of stripy fur all dirty and mussed. My tiny, fat-bellied, wriggly kitten with the very pink feet and the little pink nose. My grown-up young cat with his white, white vest, yowling and clinging to the front door. And the tomcat who had raised his kittens. Was this, then, how life ended? This was death? This ugliness and suffering? I scowled through my tears. There was such a weary yet rigid look to him. He cared for nothing now, had already gone away from me, from everything, to some dark emptiness of not being where I could neither follow nor call him back.

Mother watched over him while I was at school down town. I sat there in my fourth grade class on the second floor of the old building of yellowish tan bricks. I was a diligent student, but there was no reality just then in my classroom. My gaze was pulled through the walls, up the hill, and onto the back terrace to rest on Pinky, to somehow hold him back.

On the second day that Mother picked me up after school, I opened the car door and slid onto the seat. And I knew —I just knew — even before I set down my lunch box. I glanced at Mother's face. She nodded and breathed out slowly. "Pinky died this morning, Sandra girl. He's there on the terrace, wrapped in towels."

I wanted to know if I could see him.

"I don't think that would be a good idea. Wouldn't it be better to remember him alive? The way he used to be? Not the way he is now?"

Yes, I thought. That would be better.

In silence we went up the hill to home.

8

SOWING,
REAPING

The week has evaporated in a flurry of lesson plans and students, and now it is Saturday. The morning sees me lingering in my kitchen, a mug of coffee burning against my hands. I wait for the dawn behind Mount Diablo. The silvered light concentrates behind the mountain; it gathers first into lemon yellow and then into deep orange. The mountain becomes a twin-peaked silhouette as the pillowy undersides of the clouds are lit with soft fire and gray shadows. A molten sphere of gold rises, is blinding, and slides up to disappear behind the cloud layer, drawing with it like a magnet all the sunrise colors. I can never tire of this cosmic event; it is always powerful, endlessly varied, a brief, silent symphony.

There is work ahead, I sigh to myself, reluctant to break the spell. I must wash the dishes, do the laundry, clean the dining room, get a start on lesson plans. I glance at Mo, who has sat down in front of the stove and is industriously involved in an after breakfast wash. "But first, Mo Man," his white forepaw stops next to his wide, white chest, his narrow eyes intent on my face, "it's grooming time."

From the little cabinet at the head of the basement stairs I gather up the flea powder and Mo's bright blue comb, and go out to the front porch. On the left, next to the chimney, I have a small, round, metal table. It was old and rusty when I acquired it, but after a good scrubbing with a wire brush, an application of metal primer, and two coats of robin's egg blue paint, it is a cheerful spot to set down my portfolio or grocery bag while I fumble with the door key. Once a week it becomes Mo's grooming table, and this is where I now set his comb and the black and white cylinder of flea powder with its top flipped up. I go back in for Mo, and tell him how great it will feel to be combed and protected from fleas. He is not being deceived, and I feel him tense up as we step out the door.

I set him on the table and cuddle him, making soothing sounds and rubbing him behind his ears. He hunkers down, blinking and shrinking away from the container of flea powder. He hates it. I remove it to the brick floor. He relaxes and presses upward into the comb between his ears. Supporting his chest with my left hand I comb with my right down his neck, his spine, the base of his tail and the tail, too. I keep up a stream of praise and chit-chat. He tilts his head back, eyes half closed, and it is easy to imagine a smile widening on his white muzzle. My face is near his, and he pokes his nose up to touch mine. "Hi, sweet pea." The comb is crammed with the thick velvet of his fur.

As I reach for the powder, he gathers himself and tries to leap off the table. "Hang in there, Mo," I urge, and I get a grip on the nape of his neck. With my other hand I shake powder all over him, and rub it into his coat. He rears and plunges like a miniature bronco, front legs spread wide. My left hand is locked onto his nape and rides him out, offering no resistance, going with the whipping of his sturdy body. "Whoa, Mosey, whoa there, little man. We're almost done." I pick up his comb to smooth his coat down, he relaxes, and I have to smile at him. For all his struggling, he never hisses, never tries to bite or scratch his way to freedom with a nasty flash of temper. How different is today from that long ago summer afternoon here with Timmy. It was the day before he disappeared, his story unfinished.

Timmy. At a year old he was independent, aloof, not sociable or loving. His arrogant, green eyes looked through or past us as if we were not worth even his contempt. He was all the reasons why people who do not like cats do not like them. He also was beautiful with a long, silvery undercoat that rippled beneath his black stripes. And he was Pinky's son. I wished he would be better friends with me.

He and I were on the front porch where it was shady, and an occasional riffle of air came off the straits. He was stretched out on the cool bricks. I was crouched down and had been petting him for some time, trying to make him pay attention to me. It was hot, and he would rather have been left alone. I knew that. I knew that I was annoying him, but something was impelling me to force the issue. Facing him, I reached under his elbows and raised him to a sitting position. His ears turned back, flattening a little. With his level, staring gaze out of those green-glass eyes he looked at the moment much like an owl.

"Timmy."

No response. His eyes were fixed impassively on some point behind me. I lowered my face into his line of sight. He was like a stone.

"Timmy? Won't you play with me? Can't we be friends?" With a finger I gave him a poke on his shoulder. There was a small, whiny growl, a rising anger barely contained. I ignored it.

"Let's play, Timmy!" With my nose ever closer to his, I waggled my fingers in his face.

I did not even see it coming. His paw was suddenly just there, a claw embedded in the lower lid of my left eye, dragging it down, exposing the lining to the rude, dry air. I froze. He made a small, abrupt attempt to jerk his claw free. "Oh, Timmy," I whispered, not daring even to change my expression for fear of precipitating a panicked struggle. But he, too, froze, his trapped front leg oddly extended and his face just inches from mine. He was looking at me strangely, as if acknowledging that he needed help. Ever so slowly I reached up, softly grasped the paw, and pressed the ball of my thumb against its pad. A picture flashed into my mind in which the cat exploded in a frenzy and slashed my eyeball to fleshy strings. Timmy was immobile. His eyes — the pupils grown very large — were staring into mine. His dark pink tongue made a quick swipe over his nose, and he swallowed hard. I lifted the paw just a bit and pushed it carefully back. The claw came free of my eyelid, and I lowered his foot to the floor. He glanced at me and slunk away. I sat there, shaken but breathing again, and felt ashamed and chastened. I touched my fingers to the stinging feeling under my eye.

My hand brushes at my face and whisks away a feathery tuft of Mo's hair. "There, my good Mo, all done." He hops from the table down to the porch floor to claim his reward of crunchies and corn chip.

9

SISSY

Mo and I are in the kitchen, thinking about
dinner. My spoon clinks on the pan of vegetables I am
about to sauté, and Mo gives his hopeful, up-tilting
cry. The notes of it always astound me in their musical
sweetness and purity; they seem a Vienna Boys' Choir
voice come briefly into my presence. Rearing up now, he
reaches and stretches both front legs until they quiver,
claws hooking over the cabinet doors beneath the sink.
"Oh, Mo! You'll scratch the wood . . ."

"Oh, Sissy!" Mother would sigh in exasperation at the
growing number of claw scars in the oyster-white paint
of the drawers. But the little cat could not leave the dish
towels and hand towels alone. We used to hang them,
limply damp from their chores, over the drawer knobs to

dry, but Sissy was mindlessly obsessed by their presence, and down would come first one and then the other. It was methodical and unfailing.

Sissy was petite and always just a bit apprehensive. She had been the smallest of her litter of mostly husky brothers, but she was the one we kept. As a female, tiny, and always timorous, she had become "Sissy," and it stuck to her, an inelegant and unimaginative name for such a delicate figurine of a creature. Her round, caramel-colored eyes set off her sleek, dark coat of blue-gray over highly defined muscling. She always bore a hopeful, please-don't-be-angry expression. At meal times she was quietly expectant, and kneaded the kitchen floor, first one front paw lifting high and curling back, then the other.

And if the towels were not put away, down they would come. Trying to help my mother, I would rehang one towel on a knob, and while I was hanging the other, down came the first again. Sissy would look up, mute, seemingly apologetic. Delicately she would trod the towel, little front feet alternating, lifting high.

Mo chirrups. Mother and Sissy vanish back into another time. I swallow over the little knot in my throat, and rattle a few pellets into Mo's dish.

10

NIGHT'S
SHADOW

I was laughing and shaking the water out of my hair and eyes as I ran the last stretch up the street and across our gravel drive. From under the dripping plumbago shot the big, evil-tempered tomcat that had been hanging around off and on for the last two weeks. "Boo!" I yelled and flapped my arms and off he scrambled. The late afternoon sky was tumbled with heavy clouds dark purple with the first drenching rain of early winter, and I had been caught unprepared a good quarter of a mile down the hill at my best friend's house. I splashed up the brick walk, took the porch steps in an oblique leap that landed me on the doormat, and burst with a grin into the living room.

My parents were in the kitchen, but something was different. Mother turned toward me with a hasty, "shh" gesture. Dad was crouched down in the corner by the back door where we fed the cats when the weather was bad. But why did I have to be extra quiet? What was Dad doing? Slowly he straightened up, and he had that expression which always came upon him when there was something he wished I did not have to know. A thrill of unease pricked my shoulders. I looked from Dad's face down to the floor. Drinking from the water dish was a strange cat. It was full grown and terribly thin and dirty, and was poised for flight. The longish coat was unhealthy and bedraggled, and it clung wetly to a trembling skeleton. Another stray. But, that grayish undercoat, the black striping, in this house. "Timmy!" My hand flew to the small scar on the lower lid of my left eye.

"Sandra girl," Mother laid a restraining hand on my arm, "he's . . . he's been hurt."

Timmy looked up, and I uttered a squeak of shock. In the center of his forehead, just above those green-glass eyes, was a gaping hole, black and bloody and oozing something pinkish gray, not blood. *I must not be sick.* How could he possibly be alive like that? Where on earth had he been these months? Who had shot him? How long had he been like this? His eyes glittered in a kind of madness. Moving quietly Mother closed the door between the kitchen and the living room so that Timmy could not dart off into some other part of the house. We three stood watching him. He was drinking again, and it seemed he never would quit. He ate only a little and began to look for a way out. Those glazed eyes had a hard, frenzied look. He did not seem to recognize any of us or his surroundings. There was something in him that was implacable, robotized. Yet, he had come back. We sat down to a subdued dinner right there at the kitchen table. Afraid for Timmy, and a little afraid of him, we felt trapped along with him. It was dark now. We could hear a blustery wind whipping through the pepper tree leaves and the high boughs of the pines. The rain was stronger, and I flinched each time it spattered against the kitchen windows. Belly down, Timmy continued to dart about in search of an escape, that hole in his skull like a dull beacon. I expected maggots to fall from it. A sinister feeling crawled over me. Timmy had ceased to be our cat, or any cat at all, and was a presence so primal, so mindless, as to be alien. The rain rattled again on the windows; I winced and drew my sweater around me. Would it be safe to touch him? What were we going to do with him, for him?

The strange feeling began to fade as we talked it over and decided to shelter him in the garage for the night. It was bigger than the kitchen, and perhaps he would feel less trapped. First thing in the morning we would take him somewhere to a veterinarian. Leaving Mother to block his escape, I went to the basement for old towels and to the newspaper rack for a thick handful of old papers. In the garage Dad arranged a box up off the floor in a dark corner away from the car and the drafty windows. Together we lined the box with the papers and toweling. Nearby we set down plenty of water and a little food. We had nothing that would do as a litter tray or even dry sand or shavings to put loose on the concrete floor, so Dad decided to leave the big door open enough for Timmy to go in and out. I did not like it. What if he ran away again? Besides, if he could get out, that stray tom could get in. Well, it was a nastily stormy night; maybe he had suspended his prowls and was asleep somewhere.

In the kitchen Timmy was crouched in exhaustion, and Dad had no trouble picking him up and wrapping him in a towel. With one hand keeping the wind and slanting rain from the cat's face, he crossed the wet porch. Inside the garage he placed him in the box, where to our relief he settled down. With a final glance at the oozing hole in his head and at his staring eyes that seemed to focus on nothing, I switched off the light and followed Dad back into the house.

I went to bed and slid into a restless sleep. I was aware that sometime after midnight the wind had died to a fitful breeze, and that the rain had stopped. At about dawn I shuddered awake to the violent screams of a cat fight. It went on and on, and my heart pounded in my throat. At last, when the sun was up and the house was stirring with warmth and light, and breakfast was nearly ready, I rushed out to the garage. I held my breath, opened the door, and looked slowly around. Nothing. No Timmy. Gone. Just his empty box, the damp gloom, and the cold concrete.

For a day or two I searched the shallow banks on the uphill side of the house and poked around everywhere among the dripping leaves and shadows of the lower lot. I called and called. The silence was a void; I pushed against it, trying to deny what it meant. If I just looked hard enough.... But it was not to be. All we were to have of Timmy was a memory of his aloneness and elusiveness. Like a mirage all his life, he never could quite be reached, always withdrawing just as we thought we had a chance with him. Now, like a mirage or a shadow at sundown, he had been absorbed into the night.

11

THE WAIF

In late spring Dad spent weekends working down on the lower lot. First he cut new steps into the steep adobe bank that led off the west end of the lower terrace. The bottom of the steps merged into a trail that was only a few inches wide, and which meandered down, north and east.

It always excited me, this miniature wilderness trail; it formed a narrow tunnel through the thick overhead crisscross of cotoneasters, toyons, and elderberry. Cats, opossums, skunks, raccoons, and deer kept the passage open, but we humans had to hunch our shoulders to make our way. There were two branch paths, one going steeply up to the east end of the lower terrace, the other drifting precipitously toward the paddock fence paralleling the lower road. It was here that the pyracantha and wild blackberries intertwined in a thorny, impenetrable mass. In the spring and early summer, it grew as much as a foot in little more than a week and always threatened to push the fence out of square. The rigid spines of the pyracantha sprouted all along its dense branches to an inch or two in length; they required a wary approach with heavy leather gloves.

This morning Dad had taken a saw, the hand pruners, and the long pruners, and had been cutting into this growth down at the east corner. When it was time for lunch, Mother sent me to tell Dad. I started down the adobe steps and paused by the two big toyons near the fence on my left. I was always on the watch these days for Timmy's body. That night when he had appeared like a ghost of himself with that bloody hole in his skull was months ago. I no longer held any hope of seeing him alive, but if I could find his body, there would be a sense of a closing. At the base of those two toyons in the little clearing, it was not Timmy's form I saw now but Pinky's grave. The little cross was sunken slightly askew, and the seasons had etched the wood into gray ridges. I could find, faintly, a "P" and a "k" in chipped blue paint on the crosspiece. The marker was making its own inevitable journey into the earth where Pinky was becoming the dust of other summers, sifting, slipping among the cracks. Nothing endures.

Abruptly I turned, entered the canopied part of the trail, and hurried on down to where I could first hear and then see my father at work. "Lunch is ready," I called, hoping he would not be annoyed, would not insist on first finishing the entire fence line.

"Good." He smiled. Sweat gleamed on his forehead. "Let's go up."

I let my breath out. He laid down his tools and preceded me back up the mottled path. It was always fun to be down here in our own little tangled forest. The growth was so thick, especially here near the bottom, that we could not see a car pass by just a few feet away. Like a rabbit burrowing into its briar patch, I could disappear down this path into a cozy, earthy refuge, and listen to the hum of the insects. But it could be a little scary, too. If I came down here early of a summer's morning, I was likely to find the path blocked at face level by the sticky ropes of a fat-bodied orange and black spider. She always seemed huge and menacing to me, looming there in the middle of her architectural marvel. I would shudder and hastily retreat. In the autumn I had to watch the ground for ponderous, furry tarantulas which, when startled, would raise up on their massive eight legs to an imposing two inches off the ground. I was terrified of them.

Now I followed my father and peered into the shadowed hollows among the trees and shrubs. The filtered light flickered with the movement of the leaves. Shapes formed, moved, unformed; I could not trust what I saw. I was almost back up to Pinky's grave, and was thinking of Mother's wonderful iced tea, when I caught a movement of something gray at the downhill edge of the trail. I stared. The shadow had substance, but what . . . a rat? I recoiled and peered more closely. No, not a rat. A kitten! It moved again, but in a thick, distracted way. I glanced up the path, but Dad was gone from sight.

I already knew that the kitten was sick. Where had

it come from? There were no kittens on our hill this summer. This one was maybe two months old, not a likely age to be exploring a far world alone. It seemed tame. I leaned down, slowly reached out my hand, and picked the little thing up, nestling it against my chest. A fecal stench assailed my nose. Then I saw the brown wetness on the underside of the tail and the matted fur along the backs of the little hind legs. "Oh, oh," I murmured. Carrying the youngster gingerly I scrambled up the path and hurried to the garage, where there were some large, cardboard boxes. I put the creature into one of them, closed the garage door, and flew back down to the basement. I was washing my hands and arms just as Mother, on a rising note of frustration, was calling, "Saaandraa!" Now I was in trouble; busy adults should not be kept waiting. I ran upstairs into the kitchen and sat down at the table. Mother shot me a reproachful glance. Dad said nothing. It was all right, then; they knew that next time I would be prompt.

When we were finishing the meal, I told about the kitten, and we all went out to the garage. My parents, too, took pity on the orphan. It had fouled the box with a thin trail of diarrhea, and its dark gray, short coat was soiled. The musty stench seeped into my nose. The kitten looked up at us with an open, intelligent expression, and it seemed to accept its sickness without giving in to it. Dad went back down to work, while Mother and I cleaned the kitten. We fixed a place in the dining room as a day ward, with lots of clean toweling, a saucer of water, and frequent, small offerings of soft food. At night it would have a box in the garage.

The week that followed brought to me both surprising revelations and questions for which I could find no answers. That tiny shadow of a cat, so young and alone and ill, what could it possibly know even about being a cat? Yet it — at least its body if not its conscious mind — was engaged in a silent, stoically determined struggle for its life. That struggle cut a path for my own young mind. The first time the orphan drank a little water and licked at a drop of baby food, it seemed just moments before the brown ooze began uncontrollably from under its tail. All wobbly but decisive, the baby turned, trit-trotted to the front door, and looked up in mute appeal. How did it know that piece of wall was a way out? I had brought it in through the back door, not the front. Hastily I opened the door. The baby made its way down the step to the porch and down the porch steps — each taller than it — to a spot of earth. It squatted, and the diarrhea came. After a bit, the kitten stood shakily and covered the mess. It clawed its way back up the steps, into the house, and over to its bed, where it lay down, shivering. My chest constricted, and I found I was looking at the kitten through a blur. It looked back at me out of eyes that had nothing of the usual baby vagueness. The gaze was totally adult, focused and wise.

Countless times over the next few days this entire act was repeated. When I see that kitten in my mind's eye now, I see it tottering away from me toward the front door. The anus protrudes a little from under the damp tail, which is arched weakly to one side. The little hind legs are bowed and seem naked with the wetly filthy fur pasted to them. A strange scene to inspire respect. But a profound respect, even awe, was exactly what I felt that week. But, respect for what? Even then, as a preteen, I knew that the kitten was not being "a good kitty," was not nobly refraining from staining hardwood floors or soiling rugs, when it asked to go out. So, what was my respect for? What was my awe about? Looking back I think that they were for and about life's complexities, of which this baby was giving me my first, small glimmers of recognition. There was dawning on me some realization of the depths of the behavioral constraints and directives under which we sentient creatures functioned. How very strong in that kitten was the compulsion to relieve itself according to the code with which its kind was born. As sick as it was, not one "accident" did it have in the house. How conscious were its petitions to go out? How conscious were my own daily decisions and actions? What did "conscious" mean? Were we humans mostly at the mercy of the chemicals and electrical impulses that were the product of our own coding? I looked at the kitten and felt that for me, too, a door had opened, opened onto an immensity that was new and fascinating.

Toward the end of the week we could no longer entice the baby to drink or to take any food. Too weak now to get up, it lay shivering even while wrapped in a warmed face towel. Did animals have a sense of dignity? I did not know, but even if not, it was impossible for me not to see dignity and purpose in that little creature's behavior. Such a self-contained, quiet fight it had made. No ditherings. No complaints. Not once had it so much as mewed. And even at the last, when I held it wrapped in warm cloth against my chest, it looked up at me with that disconcertingly intelligent, sedate gaze.

We had not even given it a name.

It lies now on the hill at the base of the two toyons, next to Pinky.

SUMMER
1946 ~ 1967

12

BRASS

Horses. Summertime. Sixth grade looming in September. But most important were the horses. At the bottom of the steep, narrow valley across the street south of us, our next-door neighbors, Doc and Gerry Coates, finished their two big white barns. My heart thudded in my ears when the first of two truckloads of quarter horses rolled in all the way from the King Ranch in Texas. For me it was an impossible dream becoming reality. I had wanted a horse for as long as I could recall, and now here, at the Rafter C Ranch, were maybe a dozen of them, all beautiful, some as wild as mustangs, and all within a minute's walk down the hill. None of them, of course, was mine. But Doc had brought me into the world, and the Coateses had always been our neighbors, so I was allowed to hang around the barns. Before long

Gerry asked me to help with the quieter mares. Here was solitude. Here were breezes, hot sun, dust, horses, the huge hills. Solid things, both comforting and exciting. And they were my first taste of something of which my parents were not an integral part.

There were other good things, too. The final payment was made on the house. And on the crest of the steep rise east of the Rafter C's valley was the two-story red barn. It had heavy double doors below and a grand hayloft above, and between the two a huge "2-H" brand in metal tubing painted orange. A solid structure, the Honegger brothers' barn stood behind a sentinel row of tall eucalyptus trees with great peels of pastel bark and sharp-scented seeds like small sleigh bells. The trees and the barn formed our horizon on that hill. All through my teen years I kept my horse there, as did several other neighborhood youngsters, including my best friend.

This was a working stable; we kids did all our own barn chores. Daily, regardless of weather, we mucked out our stalls and corrals. In the chilly, marvelous dawns every day before school we ran up to the barn to check the water and feed the hay we had laid out the night before on burlap sacks by our stall doors. The early light gave everything separate significance: Mount Diablo in the distance stood out against the translucent sky; the bluish dappling of the eucalyptus leaves lay lightly on the barn's red roof and walls and on the hard earth; the manes of the horses shone, and the muscling of their legs was softly sculpted with shadow. The air, too, was alive. I filled my lungs with the sweetness of the hay and the sharpness of the eucalyptus. The dust of the corrals, dew-dampened, smelled musky and clean. This place, these things, the earth contact through the horses, were becoming my center, a boundless well of both peace and high adventure.

We kids rode after school and weekends, mostly bareback and often at a gallop, all over the hills for miles around. In the summer we rode all day and into the twilight. Often after dark we rode on hills turned to muted gold and silver velvet beneath a moon gone all orangey and as huge as the Earth. When we moved cattle for Doc and Gerry, we had to saddle up and ride soberly and early in the day. On the ridge lines our horses clung then to deer trails and cow trails, just narrow ledges carved by hooves on the steep faces of grass-slick hills. Below us in the still air a turkey buzzard or two floated high above the tops of laurel and oak down in the canyon shadows. The strong light struck a brownish sheen on the great, spread wings. Magnificent creatures, I always thought; they were the essence of grace, elegance, and quiet purpose.

But the teen years were soon over, and a driver's license marked my entry into a different life. Somehow my university education with its grinding, trying times was soon behind me, too. My teaching credential was in my file, a Phi Beta Kappa key was tucked away somewhere in a drawer, and I was teaching at Clayton Valley High School on the far side of Concord. But what was a beginning was also an ending. I thought of the wild grasses that turn all at once from green to gold on the hills, and of how I seemed always to miss the exact moment. Something of me was gone, too, swept away in the relentless blizzard of lecture notes and weekly papers and largely meaningless exams. I had entered the time of the ever increasing responsibilities and impedimenta of the grownups' world. There was no longer any time to drink from my well, to breathe of the earth, or to feel the morning air from the back of a horse. What had been would not be again. I mourn it still.

But I was, after all, young, and to my teaching I brought much energy and enthusiasm. Dad finished the east end of the basement to become my home working space. Through its two windows I could look out onto the lower terrace and on down to the straits and the hills of Solano County. It was a good place to do my endless school preparations. I spent so much time there that Mother and Dad dubbed it my "dungeon."

That particular weekend did indeed find me in my dungeon, working my slow way through a load of papers and lesson plans. For most of the morning Mary Anne had been curled in the wicker chair nearby, trying to find a comfortable position. She was pregnant with her first kittens and was restive, for the babies were moving frequently. Earlier I had watched her, thinking that she might give birth that evening or the next morning. I smiled; I had been a skinny eleven year old the last time there were baby kittens here, and I was looking forward to this event. I turned back to my work, and the hours slipped past.

When I heard Dad calling me, I looked around and saw that Mary Anne was not in the room. I trotted upstairs, stiff from sitting, grateful for the break. In the kitchen Dad was kneeling on the floor in the corner where a week ago we had put the wicker basket for Mary Anne. We had taken every opportunity to convince her that it would make a much better nursery than her favorite place under the oak desk in the top floor bedroom. True to form she had appeared to ignore the basket. But she was in it now, and her labor had begun.

Her big, round eyes, a clear glass-green like Timmy's had been, looked up at Dad and me with distress and a hint of fear. Her belly looked bloated and smooth. I could not recall that any of our other female cats had looked like this when it was their time. They had looked as she had earlier — heavy, with increasingly well-defined little shapes moving inside. We stayed with her as the minutes crept by until she expelled first one and then a second baby. She attended to them while we praised her. The births had exhausted her, however, and she lay back prone and uncomfortable. Her middle still looked awfully big; there would be more kittens, and it might be difficult for her. Poor little girl. She was not much over a year old, but the inert form lying here so quiet and undemanding was not at all like the kitten that had arrived one day about eight or nine months ago.

Working in my dungeon on a hot afternoon, I had raised my head to look out the windows and rest my eyes. My gaze was on the hills across the water when Dad appeared from the east end of the terrace. He had gone for a walk, but he had not returned alone. Sitting up saucily on his left shoulder was a kitten about six months old. It had large, green eyes with very black pupils whose look was direct and penetrating. It saw me through the window and opened wide a mouth from which ushered a demanding "Meeaaa!" Well! I had been commanded. No shy violet, this one. I suppressed a laugh as I went out onto the terrace.

"I'm afraid it's a girl," Dad said.

Maybe so, but she sat his shoulder like a cossack on his steed. "Where in the world . . . ?" I began, and reached out tentatively to her, Yes, I could pet her; that was not only permissible but expected, the homage of the subject to the queen.

"I went down to the barn." my father began. The two white barns were old now, the stalls and corrals mostly unused, the fence posts rotting in the ground. But it was peaceful, and one could sit among the grasses in the warm sun, and dream. "I kept hearing a kitten, but I couldn't see where it was. I called and walked through all the stalls, and was starting back up the road when she came bounding out of the grass."

"She doesn't seem hurt," I looked her over, " and she's sure not afraid of people."

"No, but I think she's been abandoned. I've already taken her all around, and nobody knows her."

I took her from Dad's shoulder and looked closely at her face. "Meeaa!" proclaimed the large mouth. I grinned and cradled her on my arm. Her coloring was much like Pinky's had been, a tan base coat covered with black, vertical stripes. But her stripes were broader, more like bars, and her white vest was larger and went all the way around her neck, like a bib. Her white socks extended half way up all four legs.

She was immediately satisfied with her new home,

taking over in a manner not exactly aggressive, but full of self-confidence. Demure she was not. With her irreverent attitude toward everything and her imperious dictums, she belonged in the land down the rabbit hole where, with the Queen, she might go about shouting, "Off with their heads!" In a wry moment Dad named her "Sister Mary Anne." And now here was our Sister Mary Anne, subdued and meek, abdomen ungainly and twitching. She was swallowing hard.

"She's having contractions again," Dad said. I watched her middle. Slowly the mound of her belly became tighter and moved toward her tail. She was working hard now, and I felt my own muscles pull down in response. At last the kitten began to emerge from under her tail. It was an enormous baby, long, black fur showing plainly through the amniotic sac. "Come on, Mary Anne kitty, push, push hard," Dad encouraged. "That a girl; once more now." She was blinking slowly, and as a particularly hard contraction gripped and held her, Dad took the baby between the thumb and fingers of his right hand, placed his left hand on her abdomen, and pulled gently in time with the force of her push. Out slid the rest of the kitten, and my mouth was agape. With an effort, Mary Anne tore off the sac, bit through the cord, and licked the kitten clean and dry. It had to be a boy; it was nearly as big as the first two kittens together. He was all over longish black fuzz except for a white bib, white on the muzzle, and white on the paws. He was so fat that his head and legs and feet were all tucked underneath out of sight. The fuzzy tail stuck out like a short dagger.

"Why, he looks," I exclaimed, gawking at him and

letting out a nervous laugh, "just like a monstrous bumblebee!"

Mary Anne's belly was flat now. With the first two babies already nursing and the newest one groping about on her, she sighed and closed her eyes.

13

BUMBLING

Somebody was knocking at the door. I had been petting the babies, nearly two weeks old now, and shaking my head over the bumblebee kitten. I got up and went toward the door where, through the window in the upper half, I could see just the top of silver-white hair in short, loose curls. Little Evelyn. What would she want this time? Would it be to tell us that our cat was out? Or that the front gate was ajar? I unlatched the top half of the door and pulled it open, fastening it back by the leather thong which hung on the wall.

"Good morning, Evelyn." I rested my elbows on the top of the door's lower section, and smiled down at her shining hair. She leaned back with her quick movement and raised her head to look at me with dark brown, bird-like eyes.

"Good morning!" It came out, "Good mawning!" in a frothy sputter, as if her dentures perhaps did not fit quite properly. Her wrinkled face was all smiles, and her eyes were made extra bright by thick, round glasses. Her smile vanished, and she peered up at me seriously. "Your cat's out!" she squawked in a loud voice always rather hoarse and full of gurgles. "Your cat's out in your yard!"

"Yes, Evelyn, I know. Thank you." About half an hour ago Mary Anne had demanded out, and she was sniffing around on the front lawn. "She'll be all right, I think."

"Well, you be careful," she croaked, "she might get hurt!"

"Yes, right. We'll watch her. Thanks again."

She nodded and hopped down the porch steps with her arms crooked upward at the elbow, like a child. At the front gate she turned and called back, "Do you want your gate closed? You ought to keep it locked!" (It sounded like, "Y'aughtah.") "Your cat might get out!"

I nodded, and carefully she placed the latch hook in the big screw eye.

"'Bye, Evelyn," I waved and watched her as she turned away. It would have been useless to point out that the cat could jump up to the gate and over it, or crawl under it, or "get out" anywhere else she might choose. Evelyn walked with a brisk step that rocked her from side to side, her feet in white anklets and patent leather Mary Janes. She always was clean and neat. Today she had a white, cotton blouse with short, puffed sleeves under a bright red and blue jumper that lay snug across the narrow flatness of her chest. She was going back up the steep driveway across the road. She lived up there in the white stucco house with the red tile roof, where she was cared for by a gray-haired widow close to Evelyn's own age.

I opened the bottom half of the door, and Mary Anne darted in with a "Meaaa!" The two of us went back to the kittens in the kitchen. I knelt and picked up "the bumblebee." With his startling size, and all that spiky, black fur set off by white feet, muzzle, and bib, it was impossible not to touch him.

Days passed. And weeks.

Evelyn stopped by frequently:

"Your cat's in your driveway!"

"Thank you, Evelyn. I'll get her."

"I'll lock your gate. You ought to keep it shut, you know!"

And months passed. Bumble grew and grew, and revealed ever more of his personality. He craved attention and was always underfoot. Before he was quite old enough to be neutered he was as tall as Mary Anne and had great big paws with heavy tufts of white hair between his toes. He was an abrupt and often graceless mover. He would rush affectionately at Mary Anne to rub his head against hers, but he charged like a small bull, and his head would knock against hers with a little thud. She would recoil, not hurt but not liking his lack of finesse. She would turn away, and soon we found that she was running upstairs to her private space under the oak desk. Bumble would stand there below, softly waving his plume, and stare after her with wistful, vacant eyes. We humans, however, had no such escape, and Bumble was a cat that was everywhere and nowhere all at the same time; he trotted in spurts, feathery tail up, crisscrossing in front of us, weaving between our legs. It was an unthinking, loving performance. He was ecstatic when we reciprocated with a scratch behind the ears and a little talk. But it made getting about the house a chancy affair, and in the kitchen it was dangerous. If he was outside "helping" Dad, Mother and I would know. "God damn it, cat," would come the roar, "get out the way!" Bumble, launched from the instep of Dad's shoe, would go sailing through the air. He would land with a tumble, and scramble back with his tail high, his expression eager, open, and delighted.

As an adult cat he loved to roll on the warm gravel of the driveway on hot summer mornings. Then he curled up nearby in the shade of the privet hedge, where his black coat blended with the cool shadows. When we became a three-car family and one car, usually the one mother drove, had to be parked in the driveway, Bumble began sleeping against a wheel or plopping down right at the center of the space under the car, where it was difficult to see him at all. But Evelyn, closer to the ground than we were, would spot him. "Your cat's under your car!" she would shout in a gargle and point with a sweeping gesture. "You ought to keep your gate locked!" So we took to getting down on all fours to check under the car and against the tires before we drove off.

The following year Mary Anne became pregnant again. She was healthy, her coat soft and shining. To her favorite retreat under the oak desk upstairs she had added the rocker in the living room and the big, wicker chair covered in brown burlap down in my dungeon. Her favorite play was to chase a piece of paper pleated and tied in the middle with a long piece of string on which one of us would pull. The paper was irresistible to her as we made it slither and dance up over the edge of a rug or down a stair. Her eyes huge and focused in total concentration, her rump twitching, she would spring at the toy, intent on the kill. Eventually she would seize it, disembowel it, and race off to hide all of herself except an excited tail somewhere under a chair.

But when she was perhaps a week away from having the kittens, she suddenly lost interest in everything. Repeatedly she went into labor which seemed to exhaust and frighten her, but which brought no babies. One morning we found her lying under the hydrangeas by the kitchen, crying.

"Well, little girl, it's too bad." Mother gathered her up while Dad got the car keys and I went to telephone the vet, grateful that at last Martinez had an animal hospital. Not usually a cuddly cat Mary Anne nestled down in Mother's arms and looked up at her with mournful eyes. In the driveway we were getting in the car when Evelyn came past walking her guardian's little terrier.

"What's wrong with your cat?" she sputtered, straining to keep her balance against the pull on the leash.

"She doesn't feel well, Evelyn," Mother explained, "we're taking her to her doctor."

"Oh." She bent over, her short legs straight, and peered under the car. "Where's your other cat? You might run over him!"

"No; he's in the back yard. He's out of the way."

"Do you want your gate closed? Your other cat, he might get out!"

"That's a good idea. Thank you, Evelyn." Dad started the motor, and we rolled away down the hill.

Mary Anne was home again the next day without any babies, her abdomen flat, clipped free of fur and showing a neat row of stitches. Bumble welcomed her back by butting his head against hers, but she was still wobbly and his attentions nearly knocked her over. With the cave-like refuge of her space upstairs obviously in mind, she wobbled toward the hall. Bumble crisscrossed in front of her, his great, heavy paws with their hanks of silk flashing whitely to the left, ahead, to the right. Mary Anne looked desperate. Mother rescued her, talking to her while she carried her upstairs and settled her under the desk. I distracted Bumble by getting on the floor and petting him. He butted my hand and climbed into my lap, where he purred like a tractor and drooled all over.

He was always, ecstatically, in the way. It was at its worst when it was time to get out the heavy, wooden extension ladder for the twice a year cliff-hanger of washing the outside of the huge living room window. On one such occasion Dad wrestled the ladder out from under the front porch and eased it onto the flagstones of the lower terrace. I pushed against the ladder's base while from the other end Dad walked the unit into an upright position. With the two of us struggling to hold it steady, Mother untied the pulley rope and began running the ladder up to its full two story height. The trick was next to walk the ladder, which from underneath looked like a miniature Eiffel Tower, into position, and to guide the top to rest just under the eaves two floors up. If we miscalculated, we ran the risk of the top of the ladder crashing through the windows. Bumble, who was nowhere around when we had begun the project that morning, arrived at this crucial moment, his banner floating high. In an excess of happy reunion he started his crisscrossing and leg weaving at a time when we dared not look down and had to be able to step firmly. He got a paw trod upon. We all yelled at him, and Dad finally succeeded in booting him. For a few moments he retreated.

With the ladder at last in place we stood catching our breath. Standing at the ladder's wide base I tilted my head back and let my gaze travel up and up along the rungs. The top of the ladder was considerably narrower than the bottom, which added the illusion of tremendous height to a situation with no lack of real hazards. I brought my gaze back down. Although the treads were flat and of wood, they were very hard, and years of use had given them a slick finish. The distance between them was long, so that when descending I had to grope around in space, all too aware of the unforgiving flagstones below. The rungs of the upper half, the extension part, were less far apart, but they were round rods no more than two and a half inches in diameter. Stepping on them was how I imagined it would be to walk a tightrope. Trusting them up there where it felt as if I were leaning backwards made my hands sweat. Why couldn't the windows have been made to open inward, where both sides of them could have been washed from the safety of the living room?

Mother had gone upstairs and was waiting. Dad had stuffed his pockets with cloths and a bottle of cleaner, and had started up the ladder. Bumble had disappeared. I stood at the bottom of the ladder, on the first tread, and gripped the sides to weight it and to steady it a little. As Dad stepped on the first rod of the extension section, the ladder swayed, as it always did. I clenched my jaw. He continued, moving up smoothly and quietly to keep the springing motion to a minimum. He was all the way up to the eaves now, and was washing the outside of one of the panes while Mother washed the same one inside. It was then that I heard an eager mew; Bumble was back and was eyeing the ladder. He loved climbing, and he could see Dad up there.

"No, Bumble!" I barked, and pushed him away with my foot. He ignored me, and from under the ladder he jumped to the second tread, faced forward, and reached up for the third step. One front paw and his head emerged just above my waist. With my knee I nudged him hard, and his hind end slipped off the tread below.

"Meyuu!" came the instant protest. His front claws scrabbled, his ears back and his eyes big.

"Get off, Bumble!" I yelled as close to his face as I could lean down. He dropped to the ground, gave his nose a quick flick with his rosy tongue, and trotted busily off around the corner of the house, the ladder for the moment forgotten.

"Sandra," Dad called down, "in the basement on one of the shelves of the paint cabinet are some thin, old dish towels. Would you get three of them for me, please?"

"Sure. Right away." I tried to quell a little rush of adrenalin. I would have to crawl with the cloths half way up the ladder, and Dad would have to descend several rungs and reach down as I reached up to hand him the rags. I tried to not think about it. Carefully I took the one long step down to the flagstones and went inside. Dad stayed up there, very still. Inside, I was pawing wildly through a pile of cloths; I could not locate the towels and the seconds were ticking away. Ah! There th...

"No, Bumble!" came the frantic shout. "For God's sake, NO! Get down!"

I dropped the cloths and rushed outside. There was Bumble on the ladder; he had managed the reachy spaces between all the flat treads, and somehow had climbed several of the round rungs. Now he was slipping and scrambling for a hold just one rod below Dad's feet. As he made a long, hesitant reach for the next rod, a hind paw slipped off and he was jerked hard under his elbows. The abrupt motion set him swinging by his front claws a story and a half above the stone paving. With his spine arched and his hind legs spread wide, he yowled in panic. Dad could do nothing; there was no place for him to step except on Bumble's front paws.

I started up the ladder. If I bent my knees enough to make a step, I bruised them or my shins. I turned sideways to lie against the ladder and, hugging it hard, I went up like a crab as fast as I could force myself to go. I loosed one white-knuckled hand and brought it back to wipe the sweat from my palm, crawled up two more spaces and wiped the other hand. Bumble was shrieking. Dad kept very still. At the first round rung my head was about even with Bumble's tail. I would have to go one more rung. Beyond that I could not go, because there would be too much weight on the upper part of the ladder, and the base could slip back and send us through the window. My feet hurt, and my breath came shuddering out as I crouched on the second rod. Don't look down. Hugging myself to the ladder with my left hand, I reached up with my right for the nape of Bumble's neck. I made a grab and pulled hard, out and down. With a screech Bumble made a grab for the side of the ladder just below my waist. His claws hooked both the wood and my leg. Clenching my teeth against the pain and the cramping in my hand, I started down. He clung to me and to the ladder, and kept on screaming. I struggled to drag him down the next few feet, where I could no longer keep hold of him. He dropped the remaining distance, lit with a grunt, and ran off down the lower lot.

"Are you all right, Sandra?" Dad's voice washed down over me, and my hands began to feel warm and dry again.

"Yes," I called up to him, my own voice rasping in my dry throat.

He looked at me for a long few seconds, his brown eyes almost black with concern. "Are you sure?"

I nodded quickly.

"I still need those rags," he said, with just a hint of a smile.

14

THE WHEEL

A wailing screech ripped the morning, left it hanging, and skewered me to where I stood on the lawn. My ears and heart pounded with the sound. The sun blinded me so that the driveway was a blur of shadows and muffled voices.

Suddenly I was running toward the open front gate; I nearly tripped over Bumble as he whipped into the yard with a gasping look in his wide-open eyes. He twisted toward the porch and ran as if pursued, leaping all three steps and disappearing down the east stairs.

I stepped onto the gravel. With the sun out of my eyes now and the thudding in my ears and throat subsiding, I could make out little Evelyn on the far side of Mother's car, by the right rear fender. She was waving her arms in sweeping arcs.

"You ran over your cat!" An accusing, reverberating squawk.

What cat? Bumble was just here and Mary Anne was inside. My glance flew from Evelyn to Mother, who in a daze got slowly out of the car. She looked at me out of a nightmare . . .

"You ran over your cat!" Insistent, hoarse.

. . . and left the car door open . . .

"Your black cat, he was sleeping in back of the wheel!"

. . . and stepped forward.

"I was watching you!" Squawk. Sputter. "You backed the car up . . ."

I spun, and gravel spattered out behind me.

". . . and drove right over his tummy!"

Onto the bricks of the porch in one long bound, I rattled down the steps where Bumble had plummeted just moments ago. From the direction of the basement Dad was approaching. Mother hesitated on the stairs in back of me, one hand to her mouth. A deep silence closed over the morning.

I looked down. There at the east end of the flagstone terrace, in the sun at the base of the towering clump of bamboo, lay Bumble, his black and white silks gleaming. He was dead.

From behind me came a small, anguished sob.

15

THE GIFT

_S_crish.

Skritch shrish.

I was trying to ignore these faint but intrusive sounds from just outside the front door; it was Sunday and I was desperate for a little time for myself before yet another work week began. I hunched my shoulders and felt guilty, for the soft noises were no doubt coming from our visitor cat. She had special ways of claiming our attention.

Dad was working on the back terrace, and Mother had gone to Safeway. Leaving Mary Anne asleep on the burlap chair in my dungeon, I had climbed the stairs to sit at the kitchen table with one of Mother's oatmeal-raisin cookies and a mug of strong coffee. Along with the hot drink in the oven-warmed kitchen I drank in the view of Mount Diablo. I began to feel again the touch of earth and of life.

Mary Anne, I thought into the vapor from my coffee. She was our only cat now. Her sleek presence in my dungeon when I looked up from my work was a comfort, a grounding. Last weekend, Saturday, had been a grounding, also. Getting the two ten-speeds on the back of the VW, and the three of us plus Mother's blue folding bike into it, was a chore that always taxed Dad's patience and my nerves. But the rides around the Yountville vineyards and along the Silverado Trail, the silent fog shredding off into the sapphire mornings, rang in my core like a mission bell.

The small sounds again at the front door returned me to the mystery of our visitor cat. She was tall and broad-framed, and she wore long, soft hair in a smoky fawn splashed with charcoal dots and dashes. A broad nose under owlish eyes distinguished her face. She had no ID tag or flea collar, but she was someone's much loved pet, well fed, well groomed, and happy. She had been making occasional stops at our house for perhaps two weeks, calling for a few minutes of polite and cheerful conversation on the front porch. We never offered her food or drink, and she did not seem to expect any. She delighted in the social contact; apparently to that end she occasionally brought us a lizard or a mole, sat back, and looked up out of dreamy, light golden eyes.

Those little shrishy noises! I could not be rude any longer; abandoning my coffee, I strode to the door. What would she have this time? Some unwary little mouse, probably, or perhaps a gopher.

I pulled the door open and looked down not on a cat at all, but on a duck. A duck all by itself. A portly, full-grown duck. It was broadside to me, its orangish-brown bill pointing its way north. Stupefied, I watched as the entire apparition — bill closed and wings neatly folded against its sides — tipped to its right. It began to levitate. Its left eye, unblinking and unconcerned, looked up at me. I stepped back. The duck floated into the room. Emerging just on its far side were the ears, back, and tail of the visitor cat, who looked small under her burden. A duck! The only ducks in the area belonged to George Honegger. In my mind I ran straight down through our lower lot, across the lower road, and straight down the next hill to arrive at George's back yard. This cat had carried this duck all the way up George's steep hill, across the road, and all the way up our steep hill?

I gaped at her. She released her charge and sat erect, looking up at me, her front paws together under the boa of her tail. Her eyes closed in a languorous blink.

The duck, finding itself without further assistance, twitched its feathers into place and with great aplomb waddled busily away to the bay window. It, or probably he, stood there and cocked his head from side to side to take in the view.

"Uac," came the succinct comment. He wriggled his fat tail and smoothed first one wing and then the other over his pert behind. A short, stout banker, nattily dressed and twiddling his fingers behind him, he stood in weighty deliberation.

A snort of laughter started out of me only to strangle in a sudden vision of general havoc and duck plops. The cat still sat there, alert but relaxed, awaiting developments.

"Uaaac." It was a guarded observation, no doubt elicited by the dubious motives of my crouched-down approach from behind. It was my turn to waddle to the window. But this duck was a gentleman through and through. Unruffled, his demeanor of banker contemplating a loan undisturbed, he kept his wings tidily folded as I placed a hand on each side of him. I lifted him. He looked at me out of a serious eye.

I glanced guiltily at the cat, for hardly had she brought her magnificent offering when here I was going out the door to return it.

"Uac, uac."

The duck must have been our visitor cat's gift of farewell, for we saw her only once or twice over the next month, and then she vanished altogether. I wondered sometimes what treasures she was bringing to her own human family. Perhaps they had already made the acquaintance of George Honegger's duck.

1969~1972

16

TRAITOR

Mo's "squishy ball" did not move last night. It is there yet this morning on the living room rug, where its stillness alerts me and is at odds with its bright pink and yellow pattern.

Most evenings after dark Mo and I have an indoor game with this squeezable, free-rolling toy. He charges after it, his thin, gray tail arched back toward his head, his white, bunny rabbit behind pumping him forward. From the kitchen he bats the ball into the living room; I hear him thudding over the rugs and skating out of control on open stretches of floor. Soon there follows a silence, and then a series of questioning, high pitched trills.

"I'll get it, Mo." Leaving the dishes I go to him. "Well, Mo, where is it?" He answers with another hopeful question. He stays close as I get down and peer under the loveseat, or under the tall wooden cabinet in the dining room, or in back of the hand-blown wine jug in the bay window. I find the ball somewhere, toss it for him, and the cycle begins anew to his sparkling-eyed delight. Eventually, when it disappears again, neither of us much feels like searching for it, and we go to bed.

But last evening, Mo ate only a little of his dinner, glanced at his ball, and plodded up to bed. This morning he rejects his breakfast altogether, and instead of asking to go out he heads once more for the stairs. I follow him, watching from the hall. He climbs slowly, and on next to the top step, he sinks down and curls up. I frown. Another cold? But there has been no flurry of sneezes, only this lassitude. I will keep him inside for a couple of days, and watch him.

Looking at Mo I see Mary Anne climbing these stairs that early evening long ago. For several days she had been unusually quiet, not indulging in her level-eyed walks through the house, or in her wide-mouth demands. Mother and Dad were away for a few days, so that particular Friday the house was extra quiet. Late that afternoon a thick film of cloud had come out of the southwest; in the early evening a fine drizzle drifted in silence out of the darkening sky. Mary Anne had eaten no dinner, and I realized with a start that I had lost track of her. She had seemed uncomfortable and increasingly uneasy all day.

"Mary Anne?" I hung up my dish towel and looked around the kitchen. "Where are you, Mary Anne, kitty?" No response. As I went through the living room, I switched on all the lamps and made myself exhale. Turning on the hall lights I found her climbing toward her cave upstairs. But something was wrong with her hind legs; they were not obeying her, did not appear to be supporting her weight. She had not been like that before dinner. With her front legs she dragged herself to the top, where she sank down and did not try again to move. I bounded up the steps and crouched beside her. She was hunched and rigid.

"Oh, Mary Anne, I'm so sorry, little one." What had I not seen? What had led to this incipient paralysis? She looked at me, and in her big eyes I saw a wall of pain and a certain indifference to my contact and sympathy. She normally enjoyed being among us, and she liked the games we played with her. She sought out a lap on winter evenings. Yet, our relationship with Mary Anne was like Alice's relationships with the inhabitants of Wonderland — varied and fascinating, sometimes much fun, often incomprehensible, but never was there a deep bonding, a real intimacy or mutual understanding. Mary Anne was difficult to know. I started to touch her, but stopped. Especially now, in pain, perhaps she would not want it.

I glanced at my watch. It was ten after six; the veterinary hospital would be closed. I flew downstairs, through the bedroom, and down the basement stairs. Grabbing a wad of old towels, I lined the cat carrier, and ran back up. Using the telephone book, I began calling one clinic after another. The minutes slipped away in unanswered ringing. What was I to do? Tomorrow was Saturday, and I could not imagine what might happen by Monday. I was listening to the interminable ringing and running my finger down the Yellow Pages when into my ear a fatigued male voice grated, "Hello?"

"Are you still open?" I held my breath.

"Not really. We close at five thirty, but an emergency kept me here. I was just going out the door."

"I have a very sick cat. I . . . I don't think she can wait until Monday."

Silence. I squirmed.

"All right. Where are you now?"

I told him and he asked, "Can you make it in half an hour?"

The hospital was somewhere on Meadow Lane in Concord, about ten miles away. A hazy memory of meadows and sunshine, of a tiny, green-banked creek, flitted across my mind. I knew where those meadows were, or at least where they might have been. "Yes," I answered, determined not to reveal my uncertainty. "I'm leaving right now."

I ran upstairs to where Mary Anne was huddled. Talking to her all the time I took the nape of her neck in my right hand, slid my left under both hind legs, and lifted her. No protest.

"Good girl, Mary Anne. Good girl." I went down the stairs as smoothly as I could, trying not to jar her. To get her into the carrier, however, I had to push a bit on her tail.

"Meeaa!" It ended on a hiss.

"I'm sorry, little girl," I winced. "I'm sorry."

With the carrier bumping a little against my leg, I started down the front walk to my car in the driveway. A mild rain dampened my face and hair. I glanced at the sky; I had forgotten the weather. I placed the carrier on the front seat, and we headed for the southwest side of Concord. The windshield wipers moved on low, and the headlights reflected a watery yellow sheen from the rain-filmed road. Mary Anne was yowling. I kept up a stream of reassuring talk.

"It's okay, Mary Anne, kitty. It's okay. We'll be there before long. It's okay, little girl."

It became a litany. I said it over and over, my right hand on the mesh of the carrier, while the windshield wipers beat a slow "thwick, thwick," between the dark and the thin illumination of the instrument panel. Twisting up through me was an increasing unease. "Meadow Lane." It was so many years ago. Maybe that land — those green and golden fields, the water gurgling along its meandering course, the old farm house way back there in a scatter of ancient oaks — maybe all that had never been on "Meadow Lane." Concord was growing so fast. Would I recognize where I was? The glow from the dashboard clock said we had only five minutes left of our half hour. Mary Anne yowled again, and I flinched. It seemed that it should be right along here somewhere, but in the dark with lights glaring off the wet pavement I could not find road signs. I kept driving aimlessly. I looked at the clock again; we were due there right now. Such a dark night. So many buildings and so many bright car lights. There wouldn't be so many lights in a place where there were fields and grasses and open sky. We were ten minutes late now. Mary Anne was silent at last. I glanced at her; she had her closed off, hard look.

A big intersection with signals, a red light, and a sign,

"Meadow Lane." *This was it?* The light went green and, sandwiched between cars in back and cars ahead, I drove on. It was hard to see, but I knew that if this was the place of my memory, it had been changed utterly. Had there really once been meadows here, and a stream, and a backdrop of trees? Impossible. I drove on, searching frantically for the number. We rolled past one darkened structure after another on a tiered backdrop of buildings themselves dark against the darkness. Far back, the downtown's night-glow lit the clouds.

There! A small, frame building with its lights on. I parked, snapped off the headlamps, and hurried with the carrier up the walk. The door opened as I approached.

"I thought you weren't coming. You're a quarter hour late."

I swallowed a retort, and apologized. He waved me to an examination room. While he put on the white jacket he probably had removed just minutes ago, I coaxed Mary Anne onto the cold table. She looked around with a baleful, frightened gaze while the veterinarian asked me questions and took her temperature. He palpated her abdomen and her spine and talked to her in soft, low tones. From above him he pulled down electric clippers.

"Can you hold her front end for me?"

I nodded and took her by her nape. I felt her growl. Her pupils were hard with distrust and pain. The doctor began clipping the hair away from the base of her tail, and she let out a screech that made me jump.

"She has a very large abscess." His voice bore tinily

through the ringing in my ears. "That's what's making the rounded area just ahead of her tail. It must be lanced and thoroughly drained and cleaned. You'll need to leave her here tonight and pick her up tomorrow afternoon."

I put on my jacket and thanked him. I went toward the door, and on an impulse I turned to look at Mary Anne, to say good night to her. The look of her was a shock like a small fist in my chest. Her expression was one I had never seen on her before, never expected from her. She was huddled into herself, her head cocked sideways. Her gaze hit directly on mine.

"You are leaving me," her expression said as clearly as if she had spoken aloud with a human voice. "You are going away and leaving me alone in a strange, frightening place."

She looked utterly bereft. Out of her face came such pleading and loneliness and sad accusation that I was shattered. For a moment I could not move. I opened my mouth, but I could make no sound. Gritting my teeth, I turned away out the door and through the wet dark to my car.

17

ODDS

How could there be such a blue? Cobalt and indigo thinned a little to translucence, it was intense and as fiery clear and liquid as the sun through a drop of dew. It filled two limpid wells, deep and alive and with black slits in the centers — Tai Ting's eyes.

They were round and large, those eyes, with the merest hint of being crossed, and were set in a face whose ears and chin were moderately tapered and chiseled. To look at Tai always washed me through with a feeling of rightness, of peace. His pliant young body moved as a willow branch dips in a breeze. His fur was the color of wheat, short but thick and softly springy; it looked cool if I was too warm, and sunny if I was chilled. His mask, ears, lower legs and paws, and the end of his soft, straight tail were a dusky chocolate dusted with sugar.

Beauty unmarred, however, is a thing of fantasy, and Tai had one disconcerting defect: he was flatulent. Chronically, unpredictably flatulent. When he was just a few weeks old, I could not resist holding him — such a tiny scrap of life and creamy fur — and letting him sleep all warm and secure on my lap. Sometimes we were mutually comfortable, but many were the occasions when a sulfurous emanation wound into my nostrils while Tai dreamed on. I would try to breathe by ducking my face down to exhale hard, then tilting my head back to take in a quick whiff of air. Up, periscope. It was not a satisfactory solution, and before long I would have to put him down in his little basket off in a corner, open a window or a door, and fan the air. We hoped it was a trait he would outgrow. Mother tried several gradual changes of diet on him, all of which he thought were delicious and none of which reduced the nearly palpable vapors which too often hung about him.

As he matured out of wobbly babyhood, Tai became in some ways precocious. Although he played a lot and played hard, he never came to have a favorite toy or a favorite game. Playing seemed to be a way of expending excess energy that might otherwise distract him from more mature pursuits. When he was four months old, we could see the smooth, adult form begin to emerge from gawky kittenhood; he would be an average sized but beautifully proportioned adult. At this same time he became a creature of exacting and punctual habits: breakfast at five forty-five, dinner at five thirty and then outside, the rocking chair in the living room — preferably on Dad's willing lap — at seven, bed at ten. He liked a well-ordered life. But he also was drawn at an early age to exploring the wild outdoors. The house was his center, but he insisted on being a part of the pre-dawn woods to the west and the slope below the lower road. Under the night's fading shadows insects scrabbled there, and animals scurried. By six months of age he had this, too, locked into his routine.

He had taken to sleeping at the foot of Mother's bed in the downstairs bedroom by the kitchen. Promptly at four in the morning he would jump down and go to the back door. I was usually up and in my dungeon by then, finishing up lesson plans and papers. If I did not come immediately upstairs, or if Mother did not get up at precisely that moment, Tai would begin calling. His voice was big for his size, but not strident; the sound was becoming like the deep music of a bell from some old sun-drenched adobe church. One of us would let him out and watch as he faded away into the cool, inky air.

I was always a little uneasy about those sojourns. Tai was still small and so young. There were always dangers. Even before daylight, traffic was greater on our hill than it used to be; at five the disembodied headlights of the newspaper delivery car charged unblinking along the lower road and up past the house. The chances of Tai coming to grief under its darkened wheels were not great. I was more concerned, perhaps unnecessarily so, about owls. Would an owl consider a kitten prey? The owls who lived in the woods were big birds, heavy bodied and low flying on broad, ghostly wings. They would be finishing their nocturnal hunts at just about the time Tai was beginning his day's innocent investigations. To make him stay in would protect him, but it did not seem natural. The cat, too, is a prowler and a predator. I thought of the big cats I had seen in zoos and how they spent their hopeless days in neurotic, endless pacing against their barred prisons. We let Tai go out.

There were, of course, exceptions. When he was seven months old, he was neutered, and we kept him in for a full week after that. It was hard on us all; by the second day he felt fine and he understood neither the disruption of his beloved routine nor the denial of his predawn adventures. He talked about it with increasing frustration and rising decibels. When at last we let him out, the house seemed deserted, and our ears rang with the silence. He immediately resumed his original schedule.

Since he was always back for breakfast by five forty, I had the reassurance of seeing him safely inside before I left for school at around ten minutes of six. One morning when I had been up before four to finish a stack of papers, I climbed to the kitchen in need of hot coffee. For a while it would relieve the heaviness of much work and little sleep. My muffled clattering brought Tai off the bed and into the kitchen, anxious to be out. Such a small adventurer, so much for him to see and to do. He looked up with a slow peal of his bell voice. I picked him up — he was warm cream and silk — and looked into his great eyes. How, indeed, could there be such a blue? Still holding him, I opened the back door, then set him down, and the dark closed behind him. He lived in two worlds; no human could be his companion on his early morning explorations.

I finished marking my papers. After breakfast with Mother I dressed for work. Where was Tai? He was nearly ten minutes late for his own breakfast, and Mother had been out twice to call him in.

I could wait no longer. I left the house with a feeling of dread that I tried to attribute to my accumulation of fatigue. I backed out of the driveway; as I turned down the hill I drew both a deep breath and a good look at the fresh lemon and apricot sky behind the dark blue of Mount Diablo. Early mornings, new hopes.

But this time I could not respond to the promise. I drove slowly looking along the edges of the road where it curved below the bottom of our lower lot, and along the straight stretch of the east bank of the woods, looking and not wanting to see. Something light colored was on the road up ahead at the near end of the stone wall that supported the bank. I swallowed a bead of lead that sank to my bowels, and rolled the car to a stop with the motor off. Out of my open window I looked down to my left at the pavement, at the unmoving body of Tai Ting. Somewhere a mockingbird spoke briefly in the silence while I just sat there, sat there in the dead morning with my hands in my lap. If someone should come around the curve up ahead. ... Abruptly I got out of the car and went over to Tai. There was no blood, nothing smashed but his young life, no depth any more in the wells of his eyes. I picked him up, a small, already stiffening form with the dulling hair of some taxidermist's pride, and laid him on the car floor of the passenger side. I turned the car around at the wide space at the curve and drove back home, my eyes and throat dry and burning with anger and sorrow.

Too briefly, curtly, I told Mother. I left Tai on an old towel on the kitchen floor, and slammed out of the house. The gravel spewed from under my tires, and my car leaped down the hill like a horse spurred. *Shit! SHIT!* I gulped air and groped through a haze of fury, searching for my self control. When I was a little girl, sad things just made me sad. But in my adult years I had developed an ugly streak of quick, bitter rage that was far more childish than my childhood reactions. Vile language and anger this time at death come out of season. Anger, really, at life. None of it would bring Tai back, nor salvage the day in front of some one hundred forty students over five periods, nor help me find again the beauty of living.

My knuckles cramped on the steering wheel, but I slowed the car. I drifted back, back to the ad in the local paper: "Siamese kittens. Purebred. $10.00." I had long been intrigued by Siamese. What fun it would be to have one. And how wonderful the bouncy play of a kitten — Mary Anne was so quiet these days. Mother and Dad and I talked it over, told ourselves no, and on the next day went to see the kittens.

The place was a short distance out of the far side of Vine Hill. We saw a small frame house with thin composition shingles in a gritty brown. In the hard-packed dirt yard we picked our way around a rusted bucket and an old rake with the tines facing up. Grass sprouted from two rickety steps that led to a sagging screen door. The three of us looked from one to the other, and we checked the address. A heavy set man whose shoulders sagged forward against his coveralls opened the door.

"You the folks called 'bout the ad?"

We nodded.

"I'll get the kittens."

He trudged to a small outbuilding and opened a windowless door. Out burst perhaps a dozen babies and two shy, adult females. The dreary yard became a foil for the exuberant if wobbly thistledown kittens. Mother and I could only stand there with foolish grins widening our faces.

"They're pure Siamese?" This from Dad.

"Yep. But they're half blue point and half seal point, so they ain't show quality or nothin'. That's why I gotta let 'em go cheap."

I had been watching one pretty little fellow who seemed a bit of a klutz. He was headed at an unsure trot for the steps, and now he rammed right into the bottom one. He sat down unexpectedly, and shook his little head.

I winced and asked, "What's that one's name?"

"George."

I glanced at the man's face and decided that he was not knowingly making a joke. Dad and I exchanged a furtive look and I had to bite my lip over a sudden bubble of laughter. My gaze returned to another kitten that interested me. He was thin, but there was an elegance about him that drew me. He was quick and inquisitive, and for such a baby he seemed full of purpose. I did not ask his name. We decided on him, gave the man a ten dollar bill, and got back in the car. Mother was in the back seat, Dad was at the wheel, and I was beside him with our very own Siamese kitten on my lap. We were waiting at an intersection when Dad suddenly looked at me with amusement sparking from his dark eyes.

" 'George,' " I drawled in a deep voice, and all three of us erupted in laughter. We stopped at Safeway, and I stayed in the car with the kitten. I looked down at the small, sleeping creature curled up so trustingly on my lap. His fur was an almost platinum blond with an undertone of light gold. His head and legs and tail, all of which would darken as he grew, were like sugar into which had been stirred a little dry cocoa. Only nature could work such a harmony of color and texture. A small stink reached my nostrils. I rolled down my window.

It took us perhaps three weeks to find a "Siamese sounding" name. Then, at breakfast one weekend, Dad said, " 'Tai Ting.' "

"What does 'Tai Ting' mean?" I asked, liking the sound.

"I have no idea." He grinned. "I just made it up, so I suppose it means nothing at all."

But to us it meant small bells tinkling in some exotic and peaceful oriental temple. It was perfect.

And now, today, just nine months later, Dad would bury Tai Ting in the little graveyard by the two toyons on the lower lot, where among others lay Bumble, the waif kitten, and Pinky.

My cheeks were wet. To help dry them I turned the heater fan on in the car; in another ten minutes I would be at school.

18

TRANSITION

The squishy ball shouts its pink and yellow, but it is once again motionless against a leg of the copper table. Mo is recuperating from another bout of his respiratory allergies, and this will be his fourth day of house confinement. I have been giving him his Prednisolone pills; this morning he is better.

In the sunny kitchen as I move about adjusting the simmer under my oatmeal, fixing coffee, cutting an orange into wedges, I glance at Mo. He is eating normally again, and there is only a trace of that clogged pipe sound in his breathing. When he has finished his breakfast, I squat down on the floor and arrange his rump between my knees. I have his pill in my right hand.

"Sitzee up, Mo Man." I lift his shoulders and press a little on his rear. "Sitzee up." It is baby talk, I suppose, but it has a more reassuring, friendly sound than the abrupt "sit up." He has come to associate the softened phrase with combing, which he likes, so he generally complies. This time he ends in more of a crouch than a sit. I tilt his head back, and open his mouth with my thumb on one side of his jaw and my index finger on the other. I drop the pill far back on his tongue. One chunky foreleg lifts, the toes of his white paw spread wide. I close his mouth, he swallows, and I give his throat a few congratulatory strokes.

"Good fellow, Mo. What a pro." The whole procedure has lasted perhaps three seconds. It is over. The pill is forgotten.

By tomorrow he probably will be thumping around in pursuit of his ball, but today he is still quiet. He plods about now seeking a good spot for a nap. He starts down the basement stairs, front feet down a step, then the back feet; he is moving like a furry inchworm, a stair at a time.

Watching him I see Mary Anne again. A stair at a time. She had been not just slow but also tottery.

"Mary Anne! What's wrong, little girl?" Her body had wobbled over her splayed-out legs as she swayed on a step a third of the way down. Carefully she negotiated the next space. Then she hesitated. As she reached down with a front paw, her hind legs went out from under her with a thump on the slick wood. She was falling in a sort of slow motion — thud, slither, thumpity, first one side and then the other and finally tail over head — and ended at the bottom in a little heap. She made no effort to get up.

"Mary Anne!" A quick chill brushed my spine. I ran down and touched her gently all over. She was staring, her eyes clear but reflecting the dull slowness of her body. For the first time it occurred to me that there was something more than the maturity of her eight years that was causing her to sleep so much. In the last two or three months, and especially in the last two weeks, she had been very quiet. Perhaps, it seemed now, too quiet. I thought about her asleep in her cave under the oak desk, or nestled into the deep chair in my bedroom, or tucked away into that burlap-covered chair in my dungeon. Places of refuge, of retreat. Seldom any more did she use the rocker in the busy and unprivate living room. I looked at her now where she lay as she had fallen, and there was a resigned look in her eyes.

"Come on, little one, let's get you upstairs." Carefully I gathered and lifted her. "Mary Anne!" I stared at her. Lifting her was like lifting a dry leaf. She did not look thin, yet there was no heft, almost no substance to her at all. I swallowed. She seemed without bones. Her underside was not just soft; the softness was like gelatin that had not set.

The next morning I drove off to school, and Mother took Mary Anne to Dr. Monser. He kept her to do some tests, and he called the next morning for permission to do exploratory surgery on her abdomen; he suspected a malignancy. When I returned from work in the afternoon, there was as yet no word from the hospital. I went down to my dungeon to prepare for the next school day.

When the telephone rang upstairs, Mother answered it. From the basement I could not hear the conversation, and

I ran up to where Mother was putting the receiver down slowly on its cradle. She turned, and our eyes met.

"Mary Anne," she began, cleared her throat, and started over, "Dr. Monser said her abdominal cavity was full of blood; she had been bleeding to death internally." Her quiet voice paused. "They couldn't keep her alive, Sandra, couldn't do any exploring. She bled to death right there on the operating table the moment they opened her up."

So Mary Anne had left life slowly, by tiny inches over weeks, over months, getting farther and farther away from us until at last she slipped away into nothing at the wrong end of life's telescope. I thought of the grasses on the hills in the springtime, green and tall, and of how easy it was to miss the moment when they turned golden with ripened grain. A significant moment, too brief and elusive, a mirror of life itself. You missed things, I had discovered long years ago, when you were not alert. What signal had we missed in Mary Anne? Had she been diminished and pulled away because we had left her, had not been paying attention at the right moment? She should have had many years yet. Neglect is an evil.

The questions hung there. And the remorse.

Mo has reached the bottom of the stairs, turns, and hops easily up into my office. I will keep him in one more day.

1974~1977

19

ANIMUS

The bell sounded for the beginning of lunch. Doors burst open and banged and bounced from the walls under the outward flood of teenagers in a hurry. I was tidying my desk and setting up materials for my last class when in came two girls who were not my own students. One was carrying a deep, cardboard box.

"Hello, ladies," I smiled. "What may I do for you?"

They looked at each other.

"Umm...," began the one holding the box. She glanced at her friend, who was staring at the floor. "Would you like to have a kitten?" It came out in a rush of breath.

Yes, I thought. But we already were feeding Socrates up at the old red barn, and ...

"We got rid of the rest and locked the mother — she's

kind of frantic — in the garage." Her voice was a taut wire. "My dad said for me to take this one to school and get rid of her, and not to come home till I did."

'*We got rid of the rest ...*'

Peering over the edge of the carton, I saw a tiny smudge of sooty fur the undertone of which was an orangey glow that stole my eyes. The baby was asleep. It would have fit in my hand.

"No," I shook my head. The girl looked at me with desperate eyes. "I'm sorry, but we're already taking care of three."

"Can I leave her here until after school? My fifth period teacher won't let me bring her to class. Please?"

For a long moment I stared at the girl. Her gaze dropped. The little ember slept on in the box.

"She'll be here." Placing the carton on the wide counter under the windows, I took the kitten into my life.

"Thank you! Thanks a lot!" Both girls radiated huge smiles and disappeared into the diminishing flow of the hall.

I had no class fifth period. After a hasty bag lunch and a run to the cafeteria where I explained my need for a little milk in a small dish, I returned to my room to work. The kitten finally awoke, and I could hear a small rustling in the box. I went over and picked her up: eyes of an unfocused, smoky blue; a smear of peach color on one side of the nose and a charcoal smudge on the other; stubs of black ears on an unsteady black head; back and tail black; and everywhere the undercoat in coppery peach and orange like a live coal. I had never seen such coloring. I turned her over; the little legs pawed the air and framed an underside of charcoal and apricot. I set her back in the box. Not once had she cried.

She began to explore her windowless prison. She tottered, and her tiny claws slipped and scritched, but she persisted. The box was double walled, and one inner side about eight or nine inches up had a half dollar size circle cut out of it. On this she was now putting all her attention. There was something up there, she knew, something up high. She looked and looked, and her head bobbed with the effort, but the focus would not come. She gave an uncertain little upward lunge too low and too far to the left. Another, too far right. Another, and her paws slithered down the circle and onto its lower arc. Now she had it. Over and over and over she lunged at that spot, defying it, mastering it. Long minutes later she curled in on herself at the bottom of the carton, heaved a big sigh, and fell into a sleep that not even the boisterous arrival of my sixth period freshmen could disrupt.

As this last class was ending and in the corridor lockers were slamming like shots, the kitten woke and renewed her silent assault on that circle. While I waited for the two girls not to return, I took the baby — such a quiet little thing — and introduced her to the saucer of milk. Another circle, another strange thing on which she could not focus. I dipped her muzzle in the tepid liquid. She coughed and sputtered, got a taste, and after another dip she made the connection. She bobbed her face into the dish, spluttered as the milk covered her nose, and repeated the process again and again.

What was I going to do with her? I had no business

taking her home. But how could I take her to the pound or leave her to this soulless wasteland of gritty plastic and concrete? Her face was sopped with milk, and there were little puddles and droplets of milk around on the counter. Suddenly, eagerly, she got her front legs in the dish. Finding my face strangely tight, I picked her up and mopped her clean with a tissue. I cuddled her against me to give her warmth and assurance. Assurance of what? Of death? It happens all the time, I thought. Life is cheap. One just looks away. '... get rid of her ...'

I placed her back in the bare carton. I expected, with her tummy full after a lonely day of no little shapes like her own among which to burrow, that she would fall asleep again. Instead, she raised her head and began searching for that circle in the wall of her cell, that challenge she must meet. She reached up, she wobbled, she tried a new spot, she lunged and fell back and righted herself, and finally she found it. All right! I grinned and raised my fist in triumph. Her vulnerability and her ignorance of it, the unquestioning, silent way she squared off with her world, both shamed and lifted me. I would take her home.

The wall clock jerked another minute ahead with a loud click in the empty room. It was getting late. I brought the car around to the rear of the school, and put the box with the kitten beside me in front. For a moment I looked at her, at life unconscious of its will or its purpose.

Rolling home in the traffic of the waning day, I considered my feelings. Why was taking home an abandoned kitten such a big deal? First was the matter of those two girls, or at least of the one who had had the box. She had abandoned her responsibilities because they were difficult. We had both been duplicitous, had both taken the easy way out. I had allowed her lie to relieve me of my responsibility to help her solve her problem or, perhaps more importantly, to help her come to terms with the reality that some problems have neither easy nor happy solutions.

A red light went green. My lips hurt from compressing them. I breathed out slowly, went through the change of gears, and back to my thoughts. There was also the kitten herself. We had no cat at our own hearth these days, but we felt as if we had three — old Socrates and the two baby kittens, all up at the old red barn.

The barn had been sold after George Honegger's death, and its solid, noble shape was becoming an anachronism. There were no more day-long, shouting work parties to get the heavy alfalfa bales to the loft. No kids sweated over the hay tongs and the creaking pulleys. No more rides afterwards in the bed of George's truck to Foster's Freeze. What a treat that always was — the thick spiral of white softness cold under a hardened glaze of chocolate. Nobody cleaned stalls and raked corrals, or swept the dust every day from the tack room. No water brimmed in freshly scrubbed troughs cut from oil drums. The loud laughter and shouts, the rivalries, the neighs, the shining necks and rumps of the horses — all gone. The barn stood now with only occasional and transient tenants. Windows were broken. Doors hung crookedly on neglected rollers. There were, however, two lively, sociable goats in one front stall and corral. And there was Socrates.

He had lived for uncounted years at the barn, this old, light yellow and white cat. Lately Dad and I had been going up to feed him. He was a living link to good things that had been, and there was about him a quality of steadfastness.

I slowed for an intersection and drifted back to last Friday afternoon when Dad and I had walked up to the barn. Socrates came to meet us. He walked sedately, tail up and head high but chin tucked in with the arthritic stiffness of his years. It gave him an aura of dignity. As was his custom, he met us halfway to exchange greetings, then led us into the barn aisle and to his dish in the alcove at the base of the loft stairs. When the goats heard us, they began a chorus of eager bleats. We fed Socrates, and gave him fresh water. There was nobody else about. After a little I climbed to the loft and opened the door at the head of the steps. Nothing. I glanced along the hay-polished wooden floor to where some of the alfalfa had been set into a rectangle two bales deep. Good; they were being confined. I tiptoed over, looked down over the edge of the hay, and there they were — two yellowish taffy kittens, blue eyed and wobbly, looking like they could be Socrates's great-grandchildren. They heard me and began mewling. Linda, maybe ten years old, who belonged to the goats, had found the kittens and was excited about raising them at the barn. A few feet away lay a box of powdered milk and, beside it, a spoon covered with small clumps of dried milk powder and ants. In the pen was a small dish of milk inexpertly mixed and separated now into cloudy water and chalky lumps. Some scraps of cloth had been put down as bedding. Linda would be along soon; I must not seem to be interfering with her project or frowning at her efforts.

Another red light, the last one before the freeway. I peeked into the box. Asleep at last. I switched on the headlamps in the thinning light.

"We'll be home soon, tiny girl," I said, feeling better. Mother would take to her right away.

Mother. I had told her about the kittens at the barn, and Saturday morning she had walked up with Dad and me. Linda was there, feeding her goats.

"Hi, Linda," I noted the sleek hides on her animals. "They look really great."

"Yeah, thanks!" She beamed. Then her smooth features constricted. "The kittens don't look so good, though."

"I haven't seen them yet," Mother said. "Would you have time to show them to me?"

"Sure!" She latched the corral gate and ran toward the loft stairs. "Come on!"

Dad stayed below with Socrates, and Mother and I followed Linda up the steps. As soon as the door squeaked open, the kittens began to cry. We looked down at them over the wall of bales.

"They're scrawny." Linda wrinkled her nose. "But I fix milk for them every day."

Mother's glance took in the box of powdered milk and the dish of cold water swirled with lumpy white powder. "What would you think about bringing up some regular milk, heated just a little?" she asked.

"How would I heat it up here?"

"Not here. At home on the stove, if it's okay with

your mom. And not hot, anyway; you don't want it to boil. You just want it warm, like it would be from their mother."

Linda's blue eyes widened. "Hey, yeah! And I could bring it up in my school thermos. Neat!"

Mother held the babies while Linda and I made a bigger pen out of more hay bales. Inside at one end we put loose hay and shook out the bedding cloths over that. Linda cleaned their dish.

"Where's their bathroom?" Mother glanced around.

The little girl looked stricken.

"Maybe some dirt, near their dish?" I suggested.

"Yeah. Great. I'll do it as soon as I finish with the goats."

So it had begun. Every morning now Mother took warm milk up to the babies while Linda was at school. She stayed with them a while, and cuddled them. Her efforts combined with those of the girl were already beginning to fill the kittens out and to give a soft shine to their short fur.

I was smiling as I turned my car into our driveway. With the kitten still asleep in her box, I let myself in the front door. From the kitchen Mother gave me and the carton a questioning look.

I grinned. "Homework."

20

ANIMUS
DEEPENING

"There's something wrong with her, I tell you."
The charcoal kitten had spent her first night home
in a padded basket in a corner by the kitchen table. This
morning, after wading in a little warmed milk, she had
silently begun to explore. Twice already she had scaled
her shallow wicker walls, and tumbled with a plop onto
the kitchen floor.

"She's too quiet; it's not natural," Mother pressed.

I scooped the baby away from her efforts to scale the
sheer white slab of the refrigerator. With Mother following
I took her out the back door and set her on the lip of
the stone wall. The morning was cool, rinsed with a sun
just risen from behind the mountain, and the gold light

touched fire into the kitten's coat. She looked up at us, her whole tiny body wobbling with the effort, her gaze unfocused but implacable and challenging. My face level with the kitten's, I grinned up at Mother.

"Her eyes speak for her. She's going to conquer the world."

But Mother frowned and, as always when upset, nibbled mouse-like along a fingertip. At any rate, this was the beginning of spring vacation, and I would be happy to watch the little creature. She glowed there in the sun, the orange pulsing through the black. She needed a name.

By late afternoon the sky was damp with bruised wads of moisture out of the southwest. They began to dissolve, folding and pulling toward earth. A wind came up, tore the folds, and down came the cold, gusty showers typical of springtime. That evening Dad made a fire in the fireplace, and the three of us watched the flames behind the tightly-placed screen.

That screen. It had fascinated me ever since I was a little girl and had watched it take form out of paper. With pencil Dad had drawn two nearly life-size clumps of cattails separated by a grassy slope. There was a frog off to one side. Next he had traced the pattern ever so carefully onto a sheet of burnished copper. With shears he had cut the scene out of the metal. It all had taken a very long time, but when at last he had attached the copper silhouette to the front of the screen's heavy mesh, a whole world had come to life. Watching a fire behind the screen had been like sitting on a knoll and watching a sunset flame into a lake.

Now, so many years later, the screen still cast its spell on a squally night. I got up, went to the kitchen, and returned with the sleeping kitten, where I set her down a few yards from the fire. For some moments she lay there on her belly, until the warmth and the flickering light began to draw her. She waddled off toward the brightness behind the cattails, the grass, and the frog that watched her coming. She stopped at a comfortable distance, a small black and copper cinder seeking the warmth from her brother coals of the lake.

The green and cool spring grew toward stronger light and into the ripening wild grain on the hills. Cinder grew out of first babyhood. Her eyes were taking on a brownish cast, and her legs were longer, more angular. She scrambled and darted in all directions, and she frequently vanished as if possessed of magic. We would search for her and find the tip of her tail disappearing into the narrow abyss behind the stove, or her eyes — a glitter of mischief — peering out from the cave-like fortress of a shoe vamp in a bedroom closet. At the front of the kitchen was a cabinet on whose lower shelf was a heavy, pottery pitcher in a light blue matt glaze. It was tall, over a foot, and narrow at both top and bottom. If the pitcher began rocking like something out of Fantasia, we would find Cinder behind it, her little body stretched as tall as it would go, her claws reaching uselessly for the top and skating down the hard slickness of the sides.

We wanted her to enjoy the outdoors, but for fear of her boldness and her ability to disappear, we could not yet turn her loose. Out of soft scrap leather Mother fashioned a diminutive body harness, and we tried it out at lunch time on a weekend. Mother tied the thin lead line to the lowest branch of the young oak near the back door, and set the kitten down on the flagstones. She swayed under the comparative bulk of the harness, and straps trailed like outlandish reins. We ate our lunch seated nearby on folding garden chairs, while Cinder staggered off under her burden. Her hind end flopped to the side. She righted herself, and with determination picked up a little speed. She fetched up hard against the end of her several yard radius, tumbled astraddle of the lead, and trotted off in a different arc, ears flattened and a pouty look in her opaque eyes. I squirmed in my chair. In our attempt to protect the kitten and give her some variety, we perhaps were creating the indignity of a side show. I was not, however, reckoning with Cinder's powers of adaptation and adventure. When she came to the end of her tether this time, she kept her feet and, crab-like, straining forward, she began to test the perimeter of her space.

Before we finished lunch, she had learned to climb the rough bark of the oak as far as the stone wall, and had claimed the lip as her lookout. She dove into an empty flower pot, harness and all, without even rocking it, and peeked at us over the rim. She climbed farther up and around the oak, winding her lead until it snubbed her. She slipped, the lead unwound, and she spiraled slowly down with her claws outspread in the air, and her eyes very wide.

The next weekend was clear and warm, and we set lunch out on a card table on the back terrace. Mother tethered

Cinder to the tree-like camellia bush that grew there in a rectangular tub. As we ate, the kitten disappeared into the depths of the bush, her lead line seeming to rise like a snake out of a basket. The bush shuddered and rattled here, then there, as without mercy she attacked a blossom or a bud. Suddenly there was an invisible scramble at the top of the bush above our heads. The leaves rustled, and Cinder parachuted out in a cascade of pink petals. Her harness snagged on an interior branch, and there she hung, a little above our faces. She remained suspended there, unperturbed and inscrutable. We nodded at her gravely, somehow not daring to let our laughter push up through our throats, and we finished our lunch.

If the harness gave us some measure of control out of doors, indoors — where we never harnessed her — she continued to disappear as if she had evaporated. One afternoon we called and called and checked on and in and under all the chairs and beds and sofas. We took shoes out of closets. We ran the yardstick behind the stove and then behind the refrigerator. No Cinder. In a final, frustrated pass through the kitchen, I bent to look behind the blue pottery pitcher. No kitten. But a pile of soot in the creamy white of the pitcher's interior startled me. I peered closely. At the bottom of the tall vessel Cinder lay asleep, the small circle of her body cradled against the narrow, inside circle of the pitcher. How on Earth...?

I motioned to Mother, and we left her to sleep. Even an intrepid adventurer needed an occasional refuge from the world.

21

EDGES

Behind the closed door at the Martinez Animal Hospital Cinder launched herself toward the big reflecting lamp. I pulled her down out of the air and back to the steel table. At three months of age she tackled everything, including this first routine visit to the clinic. Now she stalked a shadow on the floor. Dr. Monser came in as I scooped her back from a dive through space to the carpet.

"What a pretty baby she is," he remarked, cupping his hand over her body. He picked her up and turned her over. "No white. She's a true tortoiseshell." With that Cinder twisted over, wrapped herself around his wrist and hand, and eviscerated them. Her eyes shone with the fun of it all, but there was an intensity emanating from her that made me swallow. Ragged threads of blood appeared like signatures on the back of the veterinarian's hand and the underside of his wrist. He waited until the attack subsided. I bit my lip.

"Well!" His eyebrows lifted. "Feisty little thing, isn't she?"

It was mid June now. I finished my grades, turned in my keys, and completed my preparations for a summer in Spain. Mother was not a traveler and was happy to have the season to herself at home. She would get some of her own projects done, take care of Cinder, and visit the goats and kittens at the red barn. For Dad, on the other hand, foreign travel opened and nourished his soul, and he was going to accompany me.

It seemed that the strident ringing of the bells at school merged into the roar of the 747, and off we went. For the next nine weeks I spoke, ate, and breathed the Spanish I was teaching. I came home steeped in new knowledge and viewpoints, enthusiasms and materials, and I found it difficult to reenter the American world of Watergate winding down. Richard Nixon had just resigned. Last summer's Senator Sam T-shirts seemed to be everywhere again with that shock of white hair above the intelligent eyes and the avuncular grin.

When I saw Cinder, my breath rushed in and struck my throat. She was coming down the oak stairs, and the transformation wrought over the nine weeks was startling. She was still a kitten, but she was now a young lady kitten. Her angles and peaked hips were shucked away, replaced by a slender roundness, a sinuous and graceful symmetry. Through her charcoal and black there glowed that under-fire of copper, and peach, and apricot. She looked at me out of big, round eyes, two agates of yellow-orange.

"You are . . . elegant," I whispered.

Her eyes revealed more than a change in their size and color. She appraised me with caution, and was ready to flee if that was prudent. Cinder, prudent?

Her old spunk and determination still bloomed in her play, and yet here, too, was a change. Or perhaps not a change. Perhaps only an unfolding, a sharpening and hardening, of what had driven her silent attacks on the interior wall of the box that day at school. Her play now seemed not only to lack joy but also to be filled with anger, and was so intense as to be unnerving. When I held my forearm parallel to the floor and about a foot above it, Cinder calculated the distance, her tail lashing, and sprang. I snatched my arm away, and she would twist and land facing me again, her eyes sparking rage. If she caught me she attacked my arm with such malevolence that had she been bigger and older the scratches and bites would have sent me to the doctor. If I was too fast for her twice in a row, she quit, her tail hurling expletives, her face spiteful and sullen. Did my participation in the game make it a battle? I tried Mary Anne's favorite fun, the paper bow tied to a string. I made certain that Cinder caught it no later than the third pounce. In a frenzy she would tear the paper to crumpled shreds, jump up, and stalk away with her ears flattened. What did we have here? I could hear Mother's words, ". . . something wrong . . ." I began to wonder.

We had resumed our daily summer visits up to the barn, where the two taffy waifs, close in age to Cinder, were growing and revealing their own personalities. The larger kitten, an all-over scrambled egg color, was gracious and serious. Dad called her "Prudence." Her smaller but chunkier sister had big splashes of white setting off her darker yellow. She was a prissy little thing with a peremptory, bark-like mew, a perfect "Priscilla." Not quite half the size of Socrates, Prudence and Priscilla always came along with him now to meet us halfway up the dirt road — Prudence steady, sedate, her tail up, Priscilla eager, darting and yipping. Venerable old Socrates. How stiff and faltering was his gait this summer, but he never failed to make his dignified way to us.

Decorum was not splashing its gentle light on Cinder's path. As she grew, so did the paradoxes and stresses surrounding her. Her hostility during playtime was so aggressive that we gave up. Her fearlessness vanished, and she became extremely shy with people she did not know. When the doorbell chimed or the telephone rang, she streaked upstairs and hid away in a closet or under a bed. Yet the roaring of the vacuum cleaner began to fascinate her. She would approach its squat, vibrating lozenge tail up, and would give it a tentative caress with the side of her face, then the side of her body. Mother encouraged her with gentle talk, and soon Cinder was rubbing all around on what was to me a scarcely tolerable concretion of sound. Mother worked with her, and in another week Cinder was reaching for the heavily ridged hose, that great serpent which writhed at one end of the awful noise. Slowly, Mother introduced the small, round brush attachment, and Cinder leaned into it. The monster changed its hollow roar to a wheezing whine.

It evolved into a weekly ritual that was Cinder's total delight and ours, too. Cinder's tail waved high as the vacuum lumbered from its closet cave, and she followed it to the middle of the living room.

"Okay, Cinder girl," Mother would say, switching on the dragon. Eyes bright, Cinder would lie on the rug while Mother vacuumed her, starting at her cheek, following down over her shoulder and her side, then over her hind end. Her tail always disappeared with a thwip right up the wand. She would roll onto her back with all four legs spread wide to have the fur of her chest and tummy tugged into the round maw of the brush. When Mother lifted the wand, Cinder would look up.

"Turn over, Cinder girl. Come on. Let's do the other side." Over she would roll and give herself to the great, whining pulls against her body.

With such regular and powerful grooming her short coat should not have had a single loose hair or harbored a single flea, yet she began to groom herself excessively. She took most of her meals outside by the back door, where more and more often we found that she soon vomited what she ate, and there was usually a mass of hair with the undigested mass of food. Her greed exacerbated the problem. We knew that cats did not grind their food in the way of cows or horses, but Cinder swallowed everything almost whole. We tried feeding frequent small amounts, infrequent large amounts, free choice, dry pellets, canned foods. Nothing changed her approach. She began to lose weight. Dr. Monser suggested an orally administered product which would help the hair to pass on to the intestines and be eliminated. It reduced her tendency to vomit, and her weight stabilized.

One hurdle at a time. She was a little more than a year old now, and we felt we could no longer put off her spaying. The appointment was made, and we left her at the clinic. Something at her core turned the surgery, like her playing and her eating, into an outward-flinging battle. When the hospital telephoned to say we could bring her home, I drove down and was asked to go into one of the examination rooms. I placed the carrier on the metal table and waited for a drunkenly wobbly but awake Cinder to be brought in, and we would be on our way. But when Dr. Monser entered, he carried a Cinder who was still deep in a drugged sleep, body stretched long and limp, the grid of stitches a cryptic illustration against her shaved abdomen. I watched as he placed the little body onto the toweling in the carrier.

"She may not come around for several hours yet." His forehead puckered. "She was waking up before we were even half way into the surgery, and we did not get the results we needed from an increase in the anesthesia. We had to switch to a more potent one." He smiled and shook his head. "She's had a pretty heavy dose. Keep her warm — that's very important — and watch her. If she's not fully awake by late afternoon, give me a call."

At home we made the dining room her recovery ward. Next to the heat from the register we placed her in a box with an inviting softness of towels, and left her in the dim quiet.

It was three hours later that the twitching began.

Tiny, spasmodic tremors in her paws and around her mouth. "She's coming out of it," I said, calling Mother and Dad.

The twinges collapsed on themselves, and Cinder lay quiet again. A few minutes later her toes pulled open in sudden spasms that spread up her limbs and through her body, and flicked her eyes open and shut. For the next ten minutes she was so still that only by concentrating as I knelt there could I find the least semblance of breath. My parents stood watching on either side of the box. Mother nibbled on a finger. Then with no warning Cinder's belly jerked upwards as if a great fist had slammed into her from underneath. Her legs began flailing senselessly.

I started back and Mother cried, "What's wrong with her?"

Cinder's form deflated, and was still. Then it erupted. Her body jumped and shuddered and bounced. Her head was yanked up. Her eyes were snapped open wide and staring, as flat and dark as though sightless. Her legs flopped in all directions.

"Sandra!" Mother gasped. "She's dying!"

We could only watch. It was as if we were seeing Cinder's body, but that Cinder was not in it. Something alien was in her rag doll skin, and was flipping it about grotesquely, ridiculing and making sport of it. It went on a long time, and then suddenly it stopped. My hands were sweating. Dad was kneeling beside her. Her breathing seemed more normal, and she was blinking her eyes.

"Well, young lady," my breath came out slowly, "welcome back."

It was another hour before she could totter on a zig-zag, her hind legs collapsing to the right, to the left, through the kitchen toward her dish.

22

TARIK

It is not quite daylight. I am sitting in my favorite kitchen chair, the one where I can open myself to my front yard and to Mount Diablo. My fingers are linked around a mug of coffee. From its dark heat a tight mist of vapor curls up to tease my nose and to comfort my face. Sitting this way is a bridge I need just now to cross from one reality to another one more immediate. Thoughts of Mother — can it really be four years since she died? — and of yesterday's visit to Dad in the nursing home had invaded my dreams last night. In the predawn I awoke murky and despondent.

I look at my coffee. It is the moment, the now, life and heat. Behind it lies only what was, what can be neither altered nor continued. Ahead lies — what? Whatever yet may be in combined chance and effort. Across my mind

comes Earl; he is like a bear with his slow, rolling gait.
We are very different, this man and I, too different,
really. So unalike in direction and intensity, our strivings
pull us along different roads. One day those roads likely
will diverge irrevocably. My glance flees out the window
and seeks the mountain. Backlit in the near dawn it is
emerging a shadowed blue, a stalwart shape with its two
cragged peaks. With a determined breath I draw my gaze
back to my coffee. No man is an island? Ah, ultimately,
every man is an island.

No, Earl and I are not soul mates, but our lives have
intertwined over the past five years like the streamers
of vapor still rising from my mug. I see the chalky-blue
van, Earl at the wheel and me beside him monitoring
the flow of oxygen from the little cylinder to his mother.
She lies with the back of her white head toward me, and
from time to time she snatches one gnarled hand over the
other at the air above her. She feels herself falling, falling
away. She died the next afternoon. I see Earl's stricken face
as he takes a plane to face the tragic death of his youngest
daughter. I feel his arms fold around me at the end of
my mother's slow dying. And I see us in shared times of
sun, and sea, and peace, and laughter.

I look around and begin to note the bright things.
The sun, up now from behind the mountain, pours its
radiance over me. The floor and the stove gleam whitely.
The two small prisms at the big window are washing
everything — ceiling and walls, pine table and floor —
with schools of iridescent minnows which dart and flow.
I begin to swim with them, submerged in sunlight, my
muscles loosening. Mo sits washing his face in a halo of

light. The snowy expanse of his vest, the curves of his head
and neck and chunky forearm, lift my face into a smile.
He glances at me. His eyes are too small to be pretty, but
out of them shines his eager soul.

"Murrr—err?"

I lean away from the table and pat my lap.

"Murr—er!" The exclamation ends on a squeak when he
lands. He circles and flops down like a puppy, murmuring
busily all the while, then leans back against my chest.
His purr vibrates up and through my ears until I feel
that it is I who am purring. Ah, Mo. I stroke his gray
head and gaze out into the bright greenery of the yard.
Happy cat, my Mo.

There had been another one once that was always
happy. Joyous, actually. In my mind he is as clear now
as when I first saw him. I had been returning from the
goats and Prudence and Priscilla at the red barn, and the
kitten had materialized at the foot of the lane. With its
poker tail stabbing the air it came with a quick trot and
a stream of talk, "Oh, good morning, good morning!
Isn't the sun lovely and warm? Isn't the world beautiful?
You're a nice person."

"Well. Hi to you, too," I grinned. "Who are you?"
The kitten looked to be three or four months old and
in excellent health, its black coat glistening with a blue
sheen. Suddenly he (she?) trotted back down the road,
calling to someone . . . I froze. It was that big Irish setter
that sometimes explored our hill in the mornings. He
came briskly, his plume waving, but when he saw the kitten
headed straight for him, he stopped with one forepaw

lifted. The kitten was delighted over this new friend to be made, and increased his speed, his tail an index of unquestioning confidence in his fellow creatures.

"Oh, hello, hello," he warbled at the dog.

Hovering between laughter and horror I stood transfixed as the kitten closed the distance to inches. The dog, overwhelmed, tucked his tail and backed up, his noble reddish brow folding into perplexity over his gentle eyes. A giggle of relief burst through my held breath, and I called to the kitten. Instantly he trotted back to me. I scooped him up and he (definitely, "he") looked at me out of shining, yellow eyes.

"If Tiffany sees you, you're a goner," I whispered to the happy face. I glanced back. Tiffany lived in the big house at the foot of the northwest slope of the red barn hill. She was a German shepherd, beautiful, very feminine, and a snarling coward that killed any creature unwary or defenseless. After she had torn five of his hens to bloody lumps, the old man living at the white barn had threatened to shoot her. As I approached our own driveway another danger occurred to me — Cinder. She was always hostile to intruders, and this one was so small. Cinder, however, was not in sight when I opened the door into the living room and set the kitten on the floor.

Mother, Dad, and I watched. The youngster was instantly and totally at home, and trotted around making little soprano comments of delight. We agreed that he had to belong to someone not far away, and that he had wandered off on an adventure. How shiny black he was, like tar or licorice. Dad picked him up and held him to his chest, and the kitten looked up at him out of those yellow-moon eyes. On his vest was a spray of white hairs like a thin burst of fireworks on a night sky. For the first time I noticed the tufts of hair on the ends of his tapered ears. They were vigorous ears, alert and forward as Dad went out the door with him to walk the hill below and find his home.

Over three hours later he was back. The kitten was still on his arm.

"Nobody has seen him before." Dad's color was high from so much walking on steep streets. "I went to probably twenty houses."

Where had he come from? Who could take such fabulous care of him and then abandon him? Could we keep him? More expense. More responsibility. We talked it over while the kitten played and explored. What about the pound? My stomach knotted. I saw in my mind scenes from that television documentary about air evacuation chambers at animal control centers. I could not forget that small glass-fronted execution cell crammed with lost dogs whose terror and pleading flooded from their prune-dark eyes. The scrambling jumble of legs. The suffocation and the shudders. At last the stillness — except from the one on the bottom. That one had jerked a while longer. I shook my head. What about Cinder?

Cinder came home late in the afternoon. At two years she was dainty and beautiful, and formidable. She sniffed where the kitten had been, and sat down imperiously to wash her face. Scrubbing one eye and an ear over her paw, she did not notice the kitten when I set him down across the rug from her. But he saw her. Up went the little tail and off he trotted, piping happy exclamations and greetings. In an instant he was rising up on his hind legs to touch her nose. Cinder, astonished and looking as if she had smelled something extremely unpleasant, leaned back to one side, and unbalanced both her body and her dignity. Her ears flattened in disgust, she whirled and trotted away. The delighted kitten galumped after her.

So Cinder gained a shadow we called "Tarik," after the Tarik who in 711 A.D. led the Moslems into an eight century domination of Spain. And Cinder, like the besieged Iberian Peninsula, slowly came to terms of tolerance with her intruder. Their favorite chair was the living room rocker, and they would race each other for it. Cinder would not share the space, but if Tarik was there first, she would turn away.

Tarik proved not only his innocent faith in the good will of all others, but also his creativity in problem solving, as in the matter of chairs. When Cinder was outside and Dad on the living room rocker, Tarik would come and sit at his feet. With round, eager eyes he would strain forward and request space in the chair. But we lived here, too, and Dad would look down over his paper or his copy of Newsweek. "No, Tarik," would come the gentle admonition. "No, kitty. Not now." And Tarik would curl up on the rug.

But one early evening he went to Dad in the rocker and announced that he was hungry. Then he turned toward the kitchen and started off at a trot, looking back to see if Dad was coming. He was not. Tarik repeated the approach, the statement, and the turn toward the kitchen. Dad ignored him; all of us, including both cats, already had had dinner. But with the third attempt, my father put down his paper and followed the upraised tail. Tarik paused at the entrance to the kitchen, and Dad went ahead. The kitten spun around, galloped back to the rocker, and was curled on the still warm cushion when Dad realized that he had been duped. In a flash of irritation he strode back and stood over Tarik, then broke into laughter at the kitten's joyous expression.

The world outside the house, however, presented problems of a far more serious nature. There was that frightful afternoon when Tarik was about five months old, and I was working in the kitchen. Suddenly from out by the driveway came a terrorized little shriek and the slavering snarls of a dog ravaging some small creature. I dropped the dish I was washing, and its splintering crash punctuated Mother's screams of "Tiffany, no! "NO! TIFFANY-Y-Y!"

I banged out the back door, doubled around, and flew across the lawn to the driveway. There was no Tiffany. But about six feet up the poplar tree on the far side of the garage was Tarik, looking very small and clinging to the tree by his front claws. His hind quarters were limp, the hair damp and mussed. His head was turned to one side, his mouth open as if in a soundless wail. The raspberry tongue lolled to one side. His eyes were huge and blank with a terror and a realization that were too big for him. Dad stretched up, pried him off the tree, and cradled his small form on his arm. The kitten's mouth was locked in that gape, his eyes still wide and unseeing. We could tell nothing about how badly he was mauled. Mother backed the car out of the garage while I phoned the veterinary hospital and grabbed a towel. With Dad holding a softly wrapped Tarik, we were off. It was a short drive, but before we were half way there, a heavy stench filled the car. Tarik's bowels were emptying. The air was warm and still, so that even rolling down all the windows did little to relieve the smell.

An hour later we were home, Tarik clean and wrapped in a fresh, warm towel. He had no serious injuries, but he had been nearly and literally frightened to death. We were to keep him inside for a week and give him lots of cuddling. It was two days before the laughter returned to his eyes, and three more before we rolled up the windows of the car.

There followed month after blessedly uneventful month for both cats. Tarik grew into a sleek, lithe adolescent who found life a continuously beautiful adventure. By the time he was neutered at ten months of age, he was as tall as Cinder and as ebullient as the first time I had seen him.

From the driveway where my father and I were trimming the privet hedge one afternoon, we watched Tarik across the road by the mail boxes. He had his rear elevated and his head down, rubbing the back of one ear on the ground, simply because all was so right with his world. He talked, he rolled, he got up to face the other way, and did it all again. We could not help grinning at him, but what most entranced us was the affection and laughter that shone from those eyes.

"He'll get killed someday," Dad remarked. "He's so

heedless and trusting."

I nodded, thinking more of cars than of dogs. "Yes, perhaps he will. But won't he have had the most glorious life a cat could have? He enjoys every moment of everything."

A car turned the corner below and proceeded up the hill at the same time that Tarik got up and started to dash across the road to us. I gritted my teeth. The driver braked and shook his head as the car dipped forward and back. Tarik was safely across and focused on his people, apparently unaware of the vehicle. The driver, a neighbor, shifted down and crawled on past the house. I picked Tarik up and gave him a squeeze. Over his head Dad and I glanced at each other.

But the days went on and there were no tragedies. Although Cinder had accepted Tarik's presence, she avoided contact with him, and he had long since given up overtures of romping or cuddling with her. He played a good deal with us, and he was forever poking his nose among the plants and the hillside grasses to see what marvelous things might be there.

He loved to share his fun. One sunny afternoon when I was outside by the back door, he appeared out of the tangled undergrowth on the hill in back of the pergola. Tail up, head up, he came trotting along the walk to me. He was making a strange sort of chortling noise. As he drew nearer I saw that he had something round and very soft held delicately between his wide-open jaws. I knelt down.

"What've you got, Tarik?" It looked like some sort of tiny ball. "What the heck is that?"

I reached out a hand, and he deposited in my palm a tiny baby quail. It shook its head in the strong light and fluffed little stubs that some day would be wings. It was completely unharmed.

"Why, Tarik, I ..." I cupped my free hand over the little puff, and cleared my throat. "Thank you."

With his tail still up Tarik looked at me with joyous eyes. Full of purpose he turned and trotted back to the pergola. The ebony of his sleek coat shone with blue glints. In a few moments he was on his way back, head and tail high, chuckling around a second tiny quail. I stood there stupidly, unbelieving. He reached me and gargled a question around his passenger.

"Oh, sure, Tarik. Thanks again." I accepted the warm gift into my other hand. When was this going to end? If he discovered he could crunch them ...

"Tarik!" I began.

But I was too late. He already had turned and was on his way back for another one, and I was running out of hands. Cupping the two fluffs to my chest I somehow managed the screen door, went in, and found Mother. Open-mouthed she received the baby birds into fumbling fingers, and heard my hasty explanation. We hurried outside, and as Dad came around from the front yard, here came Tarik to present me with the third hatchling, unhurt like the others. He looked from it to me, eyes shining.

"Oh, look," he seemed to say, "just look at them! Aren't they cute? Isn't this wonderful fun?" And off he went again, his slender young form shouting his intent, "There are more. I'll get you another one!"

I groaned and deposited the latest throb into Mother's hands while Dad hurried to the attic for a shoe box. I jogged after Tarik, who gladly showed me the nest. Just one little baby left. A few yards away a rustle and flutter in the grasses revealed the distraught parent birds. And here I was, about to kidnap their last child. Tarik watched with approval as I closed a hand over the baby.

"Come on, Tarik," I called, trying to sound cheerful, and to my relief he trotted along right behind me. At the back door Dad held a box while Mother settled the baby birds into its depths. I deposited the last one and enticed Tarik into the kitchen. While Mother and Dad drove off with the box to The Lindsay Museum, where the hatchlings would be raised and then set free, I left Tarik in the house and strode back to the pergola to search for signs of other quail. Nothing. Intending to take Tarik's mind away from this adventure, I returned to the house. He was not in the kitchen, and I went on into the living room. There he was, asleep on the rocking chair, so relaxed that he could have been there for hours.

A few days later Dad found Tarik dead at the curve in the road below the lower lot. He looked alive, as if he simply were napping there among the dry grasses. We wrapped him in a white towel, and Dad cradled him in his arms back up to the driveway. The three of us stood speechless while the sun shone hard on the tar black fur and into the wide open eyes. For a long minute I looked for him far down in their yellow amber. The laughter was still in them, frozen.

Late that afternoon my father dug another grave in the

little cemetery high on the lower lot. Mother and I stood there as Dad knelt and placed Tarik's shell in the earth. He was only a little more than a year old.

The sun was falling behind the woods and the ridge of hills, and in the muted light the wild grasses dipped and swayed. A cool breeze stirred in my hair, brushed my wet face. Except for Dad's sudden sobs, life had paused and was empty and silent.

23

WEATHERING

"Oh, Cinder, not again!"

Torn between revulsion and compassion I watched her sides heave. The spasm stretched her mouth and released a large mouse, head first and whole, in a gush of slick juices. She stared fastidiously at her mess.

I sighed. This should have been the early prime of her life, but the gloss had been fading from her soft mantle, and the embers of her undercoat held no fires. What was causing this avid hunting, this swallowing whole of prey that might still have been trying to escape as it suffocated in her stomach? As I disposed of the accident and sponged the kitchen floor, I thought back a few days to when she had pounced on a lizard in the back yard. Without preamble she had swallowed it. In a few moments she vomited, and, like the mouse just now, the lizard had come head first and looking as if it might shake itself and scamper off. The week before that there had been a hefty, square-bodied little mole; I actually had washed it off to see if it was, just perhaps, somehow still alive.

Mother and I talked it over, and I made an appointment at the hospital for the following afternoon. We kept Cinder inside to assure her availability; she began to pace and to eye us with reproach and suspicion. The next day when it was time to go, she spread her claws in furious protest at the carrier. In the struggle, she tangled herself among the folds of the towel on the carrier's floor, flipped forward with the towel dragging from a claw, and lunged. I grabbed. Cinder and the towel ended in an undignified jumble in the carrier. I could feel my mouth clamped in a tight line. *Damn it, cat, everything with you is a hassle!*

As we drove down the hill, I glanced apologetically at her through the cage's wire mesh. Even now at three years of age she rarely meowed, and from the carrier came only a sustained and accusatory growl. Her orangey agate eyes were guarded and fearful, and she would not look at me. I let my breath out slowly. Always, always, she battled. Always quietly, always herself against her world. Everything and everyone seemed to betray her; if only we could build her trust, find a way to bond better.

At the clinic Dr. Monser found no fever or other indication of discomfort or disease. He stood by the examination table, his chin cupped in his hand, and looked at Cinder as she huddled under my touch. The table was a litter of her sweaty paw prints and her hairs.

"Her coat is dry," he commented. "What are you feeding her?"

I recounted the various types of both dry and canned cat foods that had filled our shopping baskets. "She gobbles everything," I finished, "but she always acts starved."

He nodded. "Many commercial pet foods appeal to the animal's taste, but are poorly balanced in nutrients — too high in proteins and fats and magnesium. Some of our pets tolerate all that better than others." He paused. "I think Cinder is simply malnourished. Here's what I suggest: . . ."

The next morning was a Saturday. Before I burrowed into my stacks of papers and lesson plans, I walked up to the red barn and into the warm, new light. There would not be many more such walks, I knew, for the land with the barn had been sold once — perhaps twice — since George Honegger's death, and I was a trespasser now in the cradle of so many of my memories. The barn stood strong and solid but coldly empty. Even the goats were gone. The cracked window in what once had been my Reno's stall splintered its captured sun. One of the great front doors hung at a painful angle. Socrates was gone. With his stoical dignity he had tottered stiffly away one morning and had never returned. Dad and I had searched for him but had found nothing. The old cat had lived with a quiet grace, and we remembered him with affection.

I looked up to see Prudence and Priscilla coming to meet me. I felt a lift, as I always did when they came into view; they were the opening of a door onto streaming sunlight, onto something alive and vital among the husks. In the front yard of the barn I listened to the water as I washed out and refilled their bowls at the old faucet. As they ate their crunchies, I sat on the sun-warmed wooden bench against the barn's front wall. To the west and south the solid, steep bulk of the hills rose in the fresh light. I saw myself on Reno there so many years ago. "Reno" because he was foaled on the Spanish Springs Ranch just out of Reno, and because he was a deep golden palomino, the color of gold coins. I saw us on these hills, buzzards hovering below and red-tails circling above, the smell of leather and horse pungent in the summer air. Now I watched the cats and listened to the mockingbirds, and when the cats finished, I started down the hill. I looked back once to see them sitting in the sun while they watched me move away.

As I crunched over our driveway, I heard Mother's car coming up behind me, and I stayed to help carry in the groceries. Cinder's groceries were there, too. I pulled out two large packages of chicken legs and breasts, and a larger than usual quantity of fresh peas and string beans and carrots. I put away our own supplies and watched Mother for a while. As she washed the chicken and put it in a pot to simmer, Cinder jumped off the living room rocker to investigate the intriguing aroma. Mother began talking to her, explaining what she was doing and why. Cinder sat in the corner by the back door, her yellow-brown gaze on Mother's face. Mother talked and talked and looked at Cinder, who looked back at her with her round eyes full of questions. A great pot of chicken was eventually cooked, chilled, the fat skimmed from it, the tender meat removed in shreds from the bones. Mother simmered the peas and carrots and string beans, then mixed them with the meat, and filled three refrigerator dishes with Cinder's meals for the week. She kept just a little out and set it down in Cinder's dish in the corner. Eagerly the cat tasted and swallowed, and with her infrequent meow she asked for more. Mother fed her tiny portions several minutes apart until she had had a complete serving. She kept it down.

And so began a ritual. The next weekend when the groceries arrived, Cinder trotted immediately to the kitchen, where she was taking all her meals now, and her eyes followed our every move, especially Mother's. Mother made much of her, talking to her and stopping now and then to stroke her between the ears. After no more than a couple of weeks her coat was losing its look of thirst, and the embers began once more to show through a soft gloss.

A kittenish devilment began to glint in her eyes. I rummaged through the cat toy drawer, selecting items she could enjoy strictly on her own terms: an openwork ball with a little bell in it, the cardboard core from a roll of toilet paper, a dingy old Ping-Pong ball. The Ping-Pong ball was the instant choice. In the evenings she had wild-eyed, tail-lashing, high-bouncing, clacking chases under tables and around chairs. We never interfered, never offered to retrieve the ball from some of its incredibly sneaky hiding places. Cinder worked out her own solutions: we would catch a glimpse of a reaching, waving paw, or of the will of Lucifer shining out of her eyes from under the couch, or of her elevated rear where her tail thrashed like a frenzied serpent. We would sputter with laughter, and double over, trying not to disturb her.

When her paroxysms of energy had spent themselves, she would head for the living room rocker. Dad found himself looking down at the mute appeal in her face, and we noted there some of the timid and hopeful apology we had not seen since little Sissy's time decades ago. "Come on, Cinder. It's okay, kitty," Dad would coax, touched by her manner. What had become of the haughtiness and the corrosive temper of her first two years? At last she would hop onto his lap and settle with her nose muffled into her tail.

The weeks of shredded chicken and lightly cooked vegetables became months, and Cinder's coat was a darkly variegated plush, feathery soft and elegant. She and Mother spent much time together. It was Mother, after all, who bought and cooked and mixed and refrigerated her meals, who talked to her, who vacuumed her every week, who knew intuitively when she wanted out. And Cinder reveled in the comfort of Mother's bed in the airy room adjacent to the kitchen. Daytimes she nested deep between the pillows, dark against the ivory spread. At night she snuggled close against Mother's feet. In the mornings Mother would wake to the feel of a soft paw on her face and Cinder's eyes, questioning, seeking her own.

All this time Prudence and Priscilla were drawing ever closer to our house. They had known for some time where we came from in the mornings, and each day now they met us farther down their hill. Then, the inevitable.

One morning when I stepped down from the porch onto the brick walk, Cinder following, there sat Prudence and Priscilla at the edge of our driveway, soaking up the early warmth. I stopped, rooted, wishing away what I knew was going to happen. Cinder froze, then streaked across the gravel. The sister cats reeled back across the road and disappeared into the downhill grasses with Cinder vanishing into their wakes.

The territorial imperative, I thought. Is there a species without it? It is a pattern necessary to the larger design, but what grief we caused when we mistook the pattern for the design. I saw myself stuffing the dried fruit into the waste can while the Fukuchis wept in the living room. I thought of how our nation, then, had treated all its Fukuchis. We had done as humans what Cinder just now had done to her feline "foreigners."

That evening Cinder came in for dinner and then, as she so often had done as a kitten, she vanished somewhere in the house. We called and called. We peered behind shoes into the unlit corners of closets. We beamed flashlights under beds. We probed behind the musty air mattresses and the Coleman camp stove in the dim recesses of the basement. Returning to the kitchen I passed the old blue pottery pitcher. No, she was far too big now to secrete herself into its ivory depths. I was turning away, smiling at the memory, when Mother motioned to me from her bedroom. I stepped into the doorway, and she put a finger to her lips. I saw nothing and glanced back at Mother, who pointed at the two pillows tucked under the oyster white of the spread. Then I saw, under the spread, the rounded hump nestled between the pillows, and the hump was gently rising and falling. I tiptoed out, and Mother switched off the light.

24

UPHEAVALS

It happened mostly while I was away.

It was my habit, as it was that of several of my colleagues, to arrive at school with the first glimmerings of morning light. Uninterrupted at such an hour, I could run copies I needed for the day's work, set up my room for first period, and become available to my students for thirty minutes before the warning bell. After the final stragglers had departed in the afternoons, I would remain at my desk in the quiet, and not leave for home until the janitor's clanks and thumps echoed down the dim hall.

So the wreckers came to our hill after I left in the mornings, and they went away in the late afternoons; the obliterating darkness came between their work and my returns. It was perhaps childish of me, but I was thankful. I knew that if I saw the red barn being torn apart, heard the shriek of nails rendered from planks whose flowing whorls and knots and weathered paint and seeped-in sun were woven into my own fiber, the dismemberment would be an ugly scrim through which all the strong, happy times would have to filter. I recoiled from that as I recoiled from the waxy manikins on display at open-casket funerals. This time, I was told that there was to be a kind of resurrection. Board after board and solid beam after beam were stacked to be trucked away to Alhambra Valley, where they would become a barn again. I could imagine it gracing one of the remaining stretches of fertile earth and green-gold trees. Children would ride and laugh and shout. Comfortably tired horses would doze in the sun, and cats would lie in the shade. Nothing endured, not forever. But this one thing at least, even though gone from me and altered, perhaps would endure a while longer.

The visions that sustained me did not reach to Prudence and Priscilla. They had disappeared at the first arrival of strange, loud-talking men and big, noisy trucks. In the early mornings and late evenings we called and searched, but there were no answering meows, no upraised tails. Then a few mornings later they appeared on our driveway only to be driven off by Cinder. The next evening they approached while Cinder was inside having her dinner. Coming to their manner were the first hints of the apprehension and uncertainty that had marked the faces and movements of all those feral cats years ago in Pinky's time. They did not belong, they knew. Their home was gone. Was there no help here? I knelt down on the gravel. They came to me; I talked to them, and pulled the stickers and burrs from their yellow fur. They looked at me, Prudence out of light yellow eyes, and Priscilla with her round, light green ones, and I saw in them both trust and a sad unease.

I heard the back door close, and Cinder was upon us in a frenzy. I started up, brushing at my knees where the gravel had been digging them, and stepped back. There was a quick, screeching snarl of charcoal and yellow and white, and all three cats streaked away.

Cinder might eventually come to tolerate them, but the days were shortening, and the nights were creeping into corners with shrouds of frost that lingered and glittered in the mornings. I looked around. Our garage? No; if Priscilla and Prudence could get in and out, so could Cinder. Could we make Cinder into a total indoor cat? I turned toward the downhill pasture across the road, and I saw Cinder's eyes the last time we had confined her to the house. No. She needed freedom to be out. I saw down into the thick, dry mustard stalks, and suddenly I felt excited. A few yards down the slope, under the sheltering limbs of a walnut tree, was the roof of the old chicken house of the Rafter C Ranch. Gerry Coates had brought in busily clucking hens just before the arrival of that first truckload of half wild quarter horses. The chicken house had stood vacant now for about twenty years. I spun and ran back to the house.

That Saturday Dad and I walked down the steep, narrow lane that separated the two pastures. In our gloved hands we carried brooms, window cleaner, paper towels, and a bucket with pliers, screwdrivers, hammers, nails, and screws. It was a soft, fall day, the gold light slanting through the dry forest of wild mustard and horseradish. Their tops moved stiffly above our heads. Priscilla and Prudence trailed behind us.

At the foot of the first pasture Dad and I pushed our burdens up under the bottom strand of the barbed wire. With some difficulty we, too, slithered up under it. The hill was steep, and the ungrazed grasses were dry and as slick as ice. We stood panting and looking up at the chicken house. On the uphill side the green roof nearly touched the ground. The downhill side was no more than half a story tall, and windowless. The east face had a white French door with all its eight panes of glass intact but spookily opaqued by the grime and webs of years. The west wall was formed partly of a shelf that was meant to be propped open in the daytime and closed at night. Outside there were remnants of a wire enclosure, which Priscilla and Prudence were investigating. The hen house stood on one end of an inexpertly laid concrete slab which with time had broken into two pieces no longer quite on the same level. We worked open the reluctant French door, and my eyes darted into every corner, upper and lower, seeking the probable black widow spiders. It was too dark inside to see clearly, and the opened door had released around me the rankly musty feel of the catacombs I once had visited in Mexico. While Dad struggled to open the shelf of the opposite wall, I ran back up to the house and brought food and dishes for the cats, and fed them on the slab.

Late the next afternoon my father and I stood back, wiped the itchy sweat and dirt from our faces, and surveyed the transformation. It had taken two days of chipping

away the ancient piles of chicken droppings in an area
where we could not stand erect, of shoring up shelves,
of replacing rusted hinges, and of general scrubbing
up. The light sparkled on the French door, and a fresh
breeze came through the propped-open shelf of the
west wall. Inside was one large box on a roost up off the
floor, and another box on the ground at the opposite
wall. We had lined both with old bath towels. We had
even scrounged up a small frayed rug to grace the cold
cement. All that was missing, I thought with a satisfied
grin, was a treacly reproduction of a needlepoint sampler
spelling out "Home, Sweet Home" for the one bare
wall. That night we fed our foster cats inside their new
house on the floor by the door, which opened and closed
freely now, and we left the shelf propped open so that
they could come and go. As Dad and I trudged home in
pleasant weariness, Priscilla and Prudence were at their
individual supper dishes on either side of a brimming
bowl of cool water.

It was nearly winter before we were aware of the problem.
Dad had been going down mornings and evenings to feed
the two cats and to check their water, and on weekends I
went with him. We would stay awhile, enjoying the feline
company and the tucked-away serenity of this little spot
on the hill. But after a few weeks one or the other of
the cats would not be there at the usual time, and finally
they seemed gone altogether from their cottage. Dad
continued to walk down both mornings and afternoons,
his hope persistent. One weekend morning there they
were, sitting in our driveway.

"Well," I exclaimed in relief, noting Dad's smile, "good morning, ladies."

They returned the greeting and preceded us down the road, Prudence moving along in a sedate glide, Priscilla in irregular spirals. She was a woolly teddy bear in yellow and white. But at the foot of our hill, instead of turning to the right down the lane toward their cottage, they continued on their way up to where the barn had been. Dad and I exchanged glances and decided to follow them. Had they found some fractured remnant of their solid old home in which to shelter themselves?

But once opposite the eucalyptus trees we could see that there was nothing remaining. The end post of what had been the first corral stood with the water pipe still stapled and wired in place. I tried the faucet. A happy burble of water pushed out a clot of glistening red-brown earwigs. Hastily I shut off the flow. There was nothing else vertical on the entire site. It was a trashy litter of rusted nails, shattered glass, a few broken planks lying about, everything partially and dangerously obscured by dry weeds. The cats were sniffing into square craters where railroad ties had once formed the corner posts of stout corrals. A few of these ties, either abandoned or forgotten, lay in a disordered scatter. Dad stepped carefully among and over the debris, and circled back to where I was standing and pulling my jacket tightly around me. The cats finished their careful, light-footed explorations, and returned to us. Neither of us had spoken. They looked up, Priscilla blinking and squinting a little as she always did in direct light. They meowed on a questioning note.

"May we have our breakfast here?" they seemed to ask. "Here has always been our home."

I looked around. Nothing. Not a stick of shelter. Nowhere to sleep. Nothing to break the night winds or the coming months of rain. I leaned down and scratched them behind the ears. I rattled my plastic container of dry food and called, "Come on, ladies. Breakfast at the cottage."

Dad encouraged them. "Come on, Prudence. Come, Priscilla kitty." But the cats lingered, sniffing at the changes, making their own kind of sense out of what was no more. Then they straggled after us down the lane.

They would not, however, enter the old hen house. We fed them outside in the sun on the slab, and while they ate, we opened the French door. There seemed nothing amiss. The bed boxes were slightly out of position, but a glance into them told us they had been little used. Why? Where were they sleeping? There were no ammoniac stenches or runny stains to indicate an invasion by some vagrant tom, nor piles of dog droppings, nor any indication of struggles or frantic exits. Thinking of this though, forced me to admit what for some time had lain unspoken at the back of my mind: the hen house could become a trap. Its very low ceiling meant no place for a cat to climb or jump to safety. The door must be kept closed or the little place would be a bleak wind tunnel, and this meant that the shelf entrance on the west side was also the only way out. Did Priscilla and Prudence simply feel the danger instinctively, I wondered, or had something happened? I pulled the water dish toward me. The water was muddied, and on the bottom were neat little furrows of sediment.

So! Raccoons had been visiting. But generations of cats and raccoons had coexisted around here and had always been indifferent to each others' presence. What else, I wondered. A skunk, perhaps, or an opossum, both numerous in the hills. There were foxes, too, occasionally, with orange-brown coats ending in thick, black-tipped brushes. Would they be a threat?

Dad and I talked about it, and then gave it up for the useless speculation that it was. What mattered was only that Priscilla and Prudence were rejecting what we had assumed to be a cozy abode for the winter. We continued to carry their meals down; they ate outside on the broken slab, and they made frequent, uneasy glances all around. More and more they spent time first at the edge of our driveway, and then in the middle of it. Priscilla especially enjoyed the stolen hours. With her chin tilted back and all four legs splayed wide, she soaked into her white-furred tummy all the thin warmth of the early November sun.

Then one day I returned from school to a strange noise in the kitchen, where Mother was preparing dinner. The heavy pine door between the dining room and the kitchen was closed, which was odd. From beyond the thick wood a quick *pit-clop, pit-clop,* met my ears. I opened the door. There was Cinder. And there was a heavy, white cast engulfing her left hind leg. She turned toward me. *Pit-clop.* My mouth fell open.

"What happened?" I blurted past Cinder to Mother at the sink.

"She went out this morning about daylight," she replied, her eyes briefly finding mine, "and a couple of

hours later I heard a scratching here at the screen door."
She sighed. "It was Cinder, and she was in pain. She
couldn't put that foot down, and the whole leg was at a
funny angle. She was trying to walk . . ."

Mother looked terribly tired, and a premonitory
vision of her in fragile old age flicked at the back of
my eyes.

"Daddy and I took her right away to Dr. Monser," she
continued, "and he said she probably had been hit by a
car. Anyway, the leg is broken. She must stay indoors,
and not go up or down stairs, until she gets the cast off
some weeks from now."

My glance went from Mother to Cinder and back to
Mother. I could just imagine what it must have been to
gather and lift the injured creature into the hated carrier,
and to make that trip down the hill. I could see Mother
holding the carrier and crooning to a frightened, hurting
Cinder. I could see my father in tight-lipped furious
silence, livid over the impending expenses and tedious
responsibilities, explosively angry with the "goddamned cat"
while simultaneously very sorry for her. Complications.
Tensions and fatigue.

Mother gave me a wan smile. "Dr. Monser said she
should heal up just fine."

Cinder house-bound for weeks. I was turning away,
wondering how we were going to weather this, when I
saw hanging over the back of one of the kitchen chairs
the harness that Mother had made for Cinder over three
years ago. She had adjusted the straps to fit the kitty's adult
form. That night, shortly before her bedtime, Mother
gently fastened the harness and the lead onto Cinder's

chest and shoulders, and the two of them made the first of the coming innumerable sojourns outside. A few minutes later Mother changed into her pajamas, lifted Cinder onto the bed, and turned out her lamp.

Hours later, as I locked up the house for the night, I turned on the front porch light and peered out the window for my usual last look around. Directly below on the threshold was Priscilla. Her front paws were tucked under her white vest, and her yellow tail was curled close against her side.

She was fast asleep.

25

INVICTUS

Painful sounds, as of metal screeching on metal, and heavy thuds on the front porch. Tattered silence. I raced to jerk open the door, and found myself staring down into startling eyes — slashes of obsidian set in pools of chartreuse like a macaw's feathers. The outer corners turned up, the lids lay level and significant. And the coat — a fall of silky fur in sweeping blocks of ermine, flame, and smooth ebony. She sat erect and serene, her tail curled over her front paws.

"Hello?" I managed, falling into those eyes, and she answered instantly in a full contralto. I looked all around on the bricks. I moved to the railing; my gaze swept the flagstones of the lower terrace, and probed into the webbing of sun and shadow that marked the openings of paths on the lower lot. No Cinder. No Priscilla. Hurrying to the front yard, I glanced under the escallonia and across the tiny meadow of lawn. No movement. I stood unsure, waiting, hearing the buzz of insects in the hot light that flowed to the shade.

I turned back to the porch, but it was vacant and silent. Where had she gone? Where had she come from? It was not unusual to have a visiting stray and, in the early spring, a few haggard toms. It was never a problem; Cinder and Priscilla put aside their differences and together drove off the strangers. But this was early autumn, and the stranger was a big female.

That evening Cinder and Priscilla were late for dinner. In the kitchen Cinder's black pupils seemed to fill her face. She ate crouched down, and darted anxious glances behind her. At her dish out back, Priscilla kept stopping to rise up and look around. Without finishing her meal, she melted away under the bushes.

Mother let Cinder out around five the next morning, but neither she nor Priscilla came for breakfast. When I stepped out on the porch to call them, there sat the calico in possession of an empire. She arched against my legs, and looked up out of those black slits in their green stones. I pulled my gaze away and looked around for Cinder and Priscilla. The calico's unabashed contralto brought my hand down automatically, and my fingers sank in the cool, floating mass of her hair. Startled by the sensuous contact, I looked at her. She accepted the touch as her due, just as she accepted the porch as the palace of her new realm in which she was to be the sole feline inhabitant.

That afternoon I opened the back door onto another

burst of snarls and shrieks, and Cinder skittered in and fled under Mother's bed. The calico stood by the stone wall with her robes settling about her in easy majesty. Bits of Cinder's fur jerked through the air and snagged among some fallen leaves. The dark hairs strained into a breeze, broke away, disappeared. I stared hard at the calico, and she stared back. She owned the world and had branded its dwellers. Priscilla had a great hunk of her wool ripped from her neck. As the days passed, Cinder moved cautiously from room to room, sniffed around corners, shied at shadows. Both she and Priscilla began to lose weight.

What were we going to do with the calico? She belonged to no one on our hill, or anywhere else nearby, and no one was looking to adopt a whirlwind. We resorted to shouting, to throwing clods of dirt at her, to turning the hose on her, all of which made us hot with shame and none of which kept her away more than minutes. We had begun talking about carting her off to the pound, and against that specter I saw that glorious coat and those chartreuse eyes.

Abruptly one morning she sealed her fate. A wail of screams again brought Dad and me running to yank open the front door. In the middle of the porch the calico and Priscilla and Cinder whirled in a knot of fangs and claws and fur. I shrank back from the savagery of the calico, and a spike of fear pierced my throat. *She's going to kill them! She really is going to kill them!* Dad was yelling and stamping and feinting at them among the eddying tufts of tortoiseshell hairs and yellow fur. I, too, darted and screamed and clapped. The porch vibrated with human and feline desperation.

Suddenly they broke apart. Holding up a front paw, Cinder vanished into the front yard, and Priscilla tumbled frantically down the steep east-side stairs. The calico remained on the porch, unscathed, and looked up at us. "Yes?" she appeared to challenge out of her level eyes. "You wished to see me?"

Neither Dad nor I spoke, but when he turned on his heel to the garage, I knew what was coming. My stomach contracted when he set the carrier down, its door open. The calico sniffed the arched entry and the towel bedding, stepped in, and turned around. "Well?" her look prodded. I dropped my gaze and busied myself with securing the cage. Dad backed the car out; I got in with the carrier tilted awkwardly on my lap, and we rolled away in a glum silence. The calico, too, was quiet, remarking the world with those cool, lime eyes.

At the southern fringe of town a brief space of countryside gave way to a scatter of light industry buildings with dull slabs of walls. At a little distance the chimney stacks of the sewage treatment plant thrust themselves into the air, rigid and soundless. From them my glance flew to the calico's clean, bright coat. Back out the window I saw the skeletal weeds that twitched where they strained from fractures in gritty parking yards. The road wound around, coiled, and uncoiled. The chimney stacks were closer, seemed bigger. A faint effluvium of human waste seeped into our nostrils. Off to my right flattened wads of faded newspaper pressed and fluttered against a section of chain link fencing. I swallowed and glanced at the cat in her cage. *The dogs in the chamber. Eyes gone huge with terror and pleading.* Elegant, confident, the calico looked about her.

The frantic glances, the scrambling jumble of legs.

Dad had shut off the motor. In front of us sat a squat building with a precise row of small windows all rectangular and blankly opaque. To one side was a heavy door with no window at all. Inside, in the gloom of cramped quarters, a man scribbled something on a paper and asked if she was tame. I nodded, and she was transferred to a white wire cage. *In the chamber the heap of still bodies.*

Dad had turned and was leaving, but I could not lift my feet. The calico filled the cage with her presence and her intense colors. She pierced me with those electric eyes.

It was my gaze that faltered.

1979

26

ANIMUS
TEMPERED

"Sandra, come quickly!"

Mother's voice. My red pen rolled away, and I took the basement stairs two at a time. I found her in the living room staring down over the back of the love seat. On one of the cushions Cinder lay licking her vest, her tongue like a shaving of radish.

"Well, what's wr…?" Cinder rolled her upper body forward and splayed her hind legs to attend to her belly. I swallowed; along her abdomen the fur and outer skin and all the deeper layers of tissue puckered open like the mouth of a pouch. With care she touched her tongue to a gash that began just below her sternum and ended between her hind legs. I groped for a lamp and held its hundred watt light down close to a laceration so straight and clean it might have been done with a knife, yet it was bloodless and as softly dry as a chamois skin. Peering closer I felt as if I were entering a cave with a lantern — past a fringe of hair at the gaping entrance, past layers of skin, and into the dim interior. I lowered the light still more, and my breath caught hard. A mass of coils pulsed and pushed wetly against a thinly stretched, translucent membrane.

"... and she seemed a little subdued and kept licking herself. Then I saw..."

I glanced at the clock. For once I had come home early from work, and there was still time to get to the hospital. Holding our breath, in an agony of fear that at any moment Cinder's intestines would burst forth in a slippery jumble, we bound her gently, firmly, in a big towel, slid her into the carrier, and were on our way. At the clinic we were settling her on the table when Dr. Monser entered and adjusted the overhead lamp. In a moment the veterinarian's expressive eyebrows rose, and he exhaled a low whistle.

The next morning, while I was at school, Mother brought Cinder home. Opening the front door that afternoon, I saw her dark fur against a white towel at one end of the couch. She lay flattened and limp in an exhausted sleep. I leaned over to watch the lift and fall of her breathing. Mother came from the kitchen to tell me that Dr. Monser had cleaned and inspected the pouch of the gash — the greatest danger was infection — and then had sewn her up. He had injected her with antibiotics and had sent home more to be given orally twice a day. She must once again be confined for an indefinite period, and we must take her in for a progress check next week and the week after. She was extremely lucky; she had no major veins or arteries cut, no vital organs punctured or ripped. A mystery. And a miracle of tissue thinly transparent and elastic.

Steadying herself on the crest of the couch, Mother turned and went back to the kitchen. I watched her with a vague unease, a feeling of things being whooshed along in an indifferent wind. I stayed to watch Cinder and to grope through my thoughts while my gaze clung to the quiet rhythm of her breathing. She was young and would recover, but the sight of her weary form was opening doors which I no longer could force shut on the passage of the years. Cinder two years ago with her back leg in a cast. And the year before that the double abscesses, one on either side of her tail. One had burst into a thick river of green with the first light touch of Dr. Monser's fingers. In the sudden stench the vet hastily had opened a screened window, and Cinder, her nostrils opening and closing and her eyes flat with disgust, had looked sharply at her rear quarters. I had brought her home with her skin cut away from two wide and raggedly draining holes. She had to swallow a dropperful of antibiotics morning and night, and had to submit each evening to a treatment like a torture. It had been important that the wounds not grow quickly closed on top but that they heal slowly from the inside out. That meant tearing through the netting of raw tissue that formed each day at the surface of the wounds. Mother and I would wrap her in a towel to leave exposed only her apprehensive face and the base of her tail, while Dad had held her on his lap. The ointment tube had a metal snout nearly one inch long; with it I had to tear through the superficial tissue and, with the probe to its hilt, squeeze ointment in a circle under the flap of the freshly opened hole. And repeat the process on the other side. My stomach had knotted each time I felt the tissue stretch and tear, and Cinder's growls and screams had drowned our soothing words. But she had been magnificent, really; she had not hissed or bitten or tried to struggle out of the imprisoning towel. Mother always had a special treat of chicken for her the moment the ordeal was over, and Cinder held no grudge, nor fear of our approach. Eventually the impossible looking craters had closed and the hair had grown back, thinly at first, and finally in its full glory.

And now this slash on her underside. How old was she? It felt like only months ago that I had brought her home from school, but it was, let's see, six years. Time. Somewhere in that whoosh Prudence had disappeared. Priscilla had stood up to Cinder and established her right to sunbathe sprawled on her back in the driveway, to eat by the back door, and at night to huddle on the thick doormat against the comforting bulk of the front porch. She had been a baby in the loft of the barn, itself gone for two years, when Cinder had been a dark smudge at the bottom of a cardboard carton. So Priscilla, too, was six. My young adult life, where was it? Vanished into that rush of wind, into twenty years of teaching — an incessant tornado and smother of work. *You missed things if you were not alert.* Mother. That slight unsteadiness of her step. And was she losing weight? I stared after her and tried to comprehend that she would be seventy-four this May.

I took in a slow breath, and focused again on Cinder. I put my hand down to her soft coat, felt her side lift and fall. I saw, truly saw, for the first time how small boned she was, and how vulnerable. Her strength was in her will. And that, ultimately, was true also of us.

I straightened up and looked out the bay window to the hills across the Carquinez Straits. I realized with a little start that they were turning green. It was nearly spring again.

27

PRISCILLA

I handed in my grade book and keys for the last time ever, and turned north out of the parking lot from Clayton Valley High School onto Alberta Way. I breathed in. The pressures withered. I breathed out, and they fell away behind me, ashes on gray pavement. Time flowed back into my veins, flowed from the soles of my feet up through my body, into my scalp, and expanded each capillary back into three dimensions. Time. I would not have to steal it, to make it up in my dungeon at three in the morning. I could pause to look around me, to see.

And that year I saw: saw time flow through the oats, saw as I had seen as a child the strong blue of the summer sky. I saw Mother and how her years were shrinking her flesh against her bones and drying her willowy form into brittle angles.

I took time to enjoy Priscilla. More and more I was helping Dad around the yard, and Priscilla always followed us everywhere, making occasional dashes at our feet and tapping us smartly on an ankle. She talked a lot, always in those yips and bleats that suited her woolly coat and her tendency to move in little jumps. Her squints and soft blinks when she looked up at Dad made me smile. And always if she was unsure, if she needed comforting, she would bury her face into my arm, and shut the world away.

She enjoyed playing with us. I cheered her on one morning as she zigzagged over the lawn, seized the birch tree, and bounded out on a slender limb. As she rode its sway, I poked a twig up to her, and she gave it a satisfying swat that sent it whirling off. Her laughter sparkled down on me through her green eyes. Healthy and clear, her left eye no longer showed where the oat head had been.

In the summers the ripened oats dropped from their stalks like little spears, and their barbed shafts insinuated themselves into the earth or into the fur or ears or eyes of the cats, and burrowed down and down. Last summer Priscilla had come home one day with her left eye closed and watering around the broken upper ends of an oat head. Gently I had pushed upward on the fur above the eye. The tip of the oat had tunneled in under the upper lid. Slippery with mucous, the upper ends of the head were crushed and bent flush with the eye's outer corner. She had been pawing at it, driving the shaft deeper. I had managed to get my thumb and forefinger around the stubble, but it had been as solidly embedded as a tree in the ground. At the hospital, after Dr. Monser had removed the barb and was explaining that the sight in that eye might be slightly impaired, Priscilla had thrust her head into the folds of my shirt against my side.

But now, late this summer, one day I did not see enough. Priscilla had been gone two days. The next morning there she was on the front porch right in my path as I juggled two sacks of groceries toward the door. Over the heavy paper bags I could barely see her.

"Out the way, Priscilla lady," I barked, the bags tilting and slipping, but she did not move. My glance caught an unnatural roach to her back, but visions of ruptured milk cartons and shattered glass distracted me. "Priscilla, for goodness sake, move!" and with my foot I hoisted her off the bricks and to one side. In a crouch I made it through to the kitchen where the sacks thudded onto the table. But what I was seeing was not the torn bits of paper in my fingers but Priscilla just before she had landed with a plop on the step: a partially expelled stool rigid under her tail, a weary stiffness to her body, a stoic resignation in her eyes. I rushed back outside, but she was gone. I called and searched and called again, and peered under bushes all around the house. Nothing. Vanished. She did not come home for dinner.

Each day that passed we looked for her, and on each our hopes faded a little more. Then late one Saturday afternoon she materialized on the porch splayed out, trembling, her fur dingy and matted and hanging on her like a dirty rag.

"Priscilla!" She did not look up or seem to hear me; all her attention was inward. She must not disappear again, I thought, must not go off to die alone and be torn apart by the buzzards. I gathered her in my arms and started into the house. Something under her was poking me; it was that log of fecal matter, or perhaps a different one, as dry and rough as petrified wood. I closed her in the kitchen, and Mother and I stood looking at her. The veterinary hospital was closed. The emergency clinic was about twelve miles away, and my car was in the dealership's service bay. Dad had the other car and would not be back until early the next morning.

Mother and I fixed a cushion in a basket and near it a litter box. I took a dropperful of tepid water and inserted it at the corner of Priscilla's clenched mouth. Drop after slow drop I squeezed the water between her teeth, stroked her throat, and watched her swallow. Mother warmed a little of Cinder's home cooked chicken and vegetables, and set a small dish of it and a bowl of water near the basket under the table. We each held her for awhile, but she had withdrawn far down into herself. We felt she would not live until morning.

But as we washed our dinner dishes, there came a change in her. She had never before been confined to a room, and she felt trapped. She yowled with startling energy, and she wobbled along the periphery of the kitchen, stretching her neck up to peer with filmy eyes toward the windows and the doors. We tried to calm her, but she seemed unaware of us. She became blindly focused on escape, and panic stripped away her animal dignity. She bumped into the legs of the table. She tried to run. She howled with a sad desperation that rose in a shriek, made us cringe, and then trailed away. She plowed through her litter box and tried to climb the wall to the big windows by the table. We could do nothing for her; we left her closed in the kitchen in the twilight gloom. What a pitiful expenditure of energy, I thought, and brushed irritably at my cheeks. She was killing herself.

It was a difficult night. The hours dragged punctuated by Priscilla's thumping on the dining room door, on Mother's bedroom door, on the back door, by her cries and her clawing at the kitchen walls. I had fitful dreams of demented animals and screeching deaths. In the predawn I woke to a sudden and palpable silence. *It's over. She's dead.* I slipped downstairs. I found Mother in an exhausted sleep, with Cinder awake and uneasy at the foot of her bed. In the kitchen I flicked on the overhead light, and shrank from the glare. Sand from the litter box was everywhere. The water bowl lay upside down, and the little offering of food lay in a puddle, its dish overturned. There were claw marks on the window sill, and in the middle of the floor lay that petrified log of feces, broken off — I supposed — at some point of struggle. I swallowed and bent to look under the table. Priscilla lay there, her eyes open. She was breathing.

As soon as Dad turned in at the driveway, Mother and I rushed Priscilla to the emergency clinic. The young veterinarian filled his fist with a twist of her loose hide, and when he released it, it stayed crumpled and lifeless. His hands under her front legs, he lifted her high above his head, and her hind legs dangled down. Her head was the only part of her with any substance; the rest was as flat and as limp as a scrap of worn sheepskin.

The veterinarian shook his head. "We're going to put her on antibiotics and on an IV to try to rehydrate her.

And we'll do some tests. If she makes it through today and tonight, you should take her the first thing in the morning to her regular veterinarian." He paused and rubbed his chin. "She's very ill," he said.

I nodded and took Mother's arm, and we went slowly back to the car. Poor kitty, I thought into the silence of the ride back. What has happened to her? I glanced out at the hills where the yellow grasses glinted in the sun, and my mind darted into corners. September was here. Tomorrow I started as a crossing guard at the corner of Susana and Pine. That and my two new private students would bring in some money until I began as a clerk at B. Dalton in Walnut Creek. Hardly a glorious career climb, but part-time employment would allow me to be at home more. I would need to be there. Things were happening, dark things that made me squirm now as we slowed to merge onto Contra Costa Boulevard. Something was wrong with Dad. What made that slight drag of his left foot? He had always been so straight, his step so springy. I bit my lip. Was I up to what I feared was ahead? *Enjoy what there is now.* I glanced at Mother as she remarked about the mall on her right. She was too thin. She sat hunched and diminished in the way of elderly people. My lips clamped together, and I looked at the road ahead with a feeling of loss, of the threads of life fraying and slipping out of my grasp to somewhere beyond any hope of recovery.

The next morning I stood with cold hands in the waiting area of the emergency clinic. A brisk young woman in a white jacket brought Priscilla out.

"She's a scrapper." She smiled. "She surprised us by

pulling through the night."

When I saw that she had regained a little of her bulk, hope flooded me only to drain away when I felt how limp and listless she was. The veterinarian handed me a card with a listing of test results and procedures. Hand printed at the bottom was, "PROGNOSIS EXTREMELY GRAVE."

I drove her directly to the Martinez Animal Hospital. Neither the tests at the emergency clinic nor the further tests that Dr. Monser ordered revealed anything conclusive. He continued the IV, and two days later he discharged her. As I took her from him, he said that the best guess was accidental poisoning, and that her recovery was doubtful.

At home Dad fixed a better litter box, and we arranged Priscilla's bed, dishes, and bathroom in a row under the kitchen table. We would take all our meals in the dining room. Cinder continued to sleep with Mother, but we fed her outdoors so that she could not upset Priscilla.

The days passed. Priscilla slept flat on her side. Her fur felt lumpy and greasy, and it invaded our noses with a heavy staleness. Every two hours during the day Mother or I eased a dropperful of water down her throat. Three times a day I filled a larger dropper with baby food — rice and lamb — and paused after every two of Priscilla's swallows until the dropper was empty. At the beginning of the second week she began to take interest in her surroundings, and then to eat and to drink a little on her own. But I held my breath; she was so weak and tottery, and still so very thin.

By the next week she was making shaky explorations

of the kitchen, and it was increasingly evident that the confinement was frustrating her. We feared she would get wild again, but turning her loose outside was unthinkable. I took Cinder's old harness and leash, and early one sun-filled morning I put it on Priscilla and carried her out to the driveway. She rolled onto her back and opened her body to the light and the warmth. We both dozed, and then I felt her rise up. She looked eagerly across the road toward one of her favorite hunting fields above the old hen house. Swaying but determined she led me across the pavement. I clenched my free hand and poked it at the sky with a little whoop. She was as wobbly as a kitten, but she was interested. She strained forward with her ears alert, and she made a drunken dash or two, floundering against the restraint of her harness.

I stood beside her, and we looked down toward the old Rafter C Ranch buildings. The cool air touched my cheeks, and the leash tugged at my hand. The dew on the downward slope of the old pasture teased a thin scent from the dried tar weed and from the stalks of mustard and horseradish. Priscilla tugged and yipped at me.

We stayed outside a long time.

1982

28

SIR PLUS

A ball of moldering yarn pushes against the palm of my hand. The ball squints up, sneezes, and shakes its head.

"Mo!" My laugh ends in a cough. "You'll smother us." His fine straight hairs waft and eddy around us in the springtime afternoon. They cling to his ears and nose and to my lips, and they hang weightless and capricious from the tight ringlets of my bang. I fan the air and bring the blue comb down to finish my task. Mo pokes his face up to touch mine. This is the second time I have combed him today, yet when he comes inside this evening he will leave a little trail of his hair. I finish his sides, his tail, and do a final stroke between his widely set ears.

"All done, Mo." I give his hind legs a couple of pats. "Away you go."

He scampers off, looking low slung, pregnant, and embarrassingly scruffy. I stand there on the flagstones by the back door, blowing my breath up over my face, and through a blur of gray and white my gaze follows him. He seems always to carry his head low, as if it were too heavy, too large, to carry high. As he pokes his way under the escallonia, his disappearing form trails the ghost of Sir Plus. It flickers, the briefest of imprints, but it has become a frequent one. I shrug; other than the large head there is nothing about Mo to evoke Sir Plus. Courtly, dignified Sir Plus.

That head, Sir Plus's head, that was all he was when I first saw him. I was hurrying down the steps from the back terrace to the lower terrace, when from the privet hedge on my right had appeared a large, disembodied, feline head. I stared. It stared back. I would not have been surprised if the face had faded around a grin.

"Hello. Who are you?" But I was on an errand for Dad and could not stay to chat. The head disappeared into the privet, and with a giggle I hurried on my way. In the press of work I forgot the incident until a few days later when the entire cat appeared. He was sitting up straight and composed when I stepped out the back door. I halted, shaken for a moment by his size; he looked twice as large as Cinder, and was tidily sculptured. I had never seen such a big fellow. He was an unremarkable grayish brown.

"Hi," I offered.

He raised his body to a crouch, ready to slip away. His eyes were cautious, but in their onyx depths shone a wish to be well received. They were round orbs in a great dome of a round head. Roached a little in tension, his back emphasized his roundness, but it was the lithe, muscular roundness of strength without the demeaning sag and blur of fat. I brought my foot forward in a careful step, and he melted off. I went on about my work. A visiting tom, I thought, passing through and checking the territory.

Days later he returned to sit on the flagstones by the back door. This time he did not discreetly disappear but remained sitting in a thoughtful attitude, and observed me as I observed him. I talked to him, but I made no move to touch him. He seemed a benign giant, but we kept Cinder inside for her meals, and we looked around before letting her out. We assumed that as the springtime waned, he would lose interest and move on. We had not fed him, had not been more than courteous to him, and both Priscilla and Cinder were spayed. But something drew him to this spot. As the days went by we were coming upon him more and more often sitting by the back door, or on the brick walk, or supine on the warm gravel of the driveway with his head raised in a gentle, lordly pose.

It was summer now, and I was sitting on the back terrace in the sun, freed for a time from house and yard chores. I let the vault of sky and the long view down over the trees to the town and the waterfront work their healing magic. Mother's opening the back door to let Cinder in brought back yesterday's daily visit by the big tom. "I think," Dad had remarked, "that we are being adopted." My glance had flown to his face to gauge his feelings.

Yes, I had thought, obviously we were. If he stayed, it meant three cats, each with a personality very different from the other. Would it work out?

From the hill behind the pergola the big fellow emerged now, as if my thoughts had conjured his physical form. He approached and sat down in front of my chair. We had not before been so near to each other, and I leaned forward to look closely at him.

"Where are you supposed to be living?" I asked. He looked at me and blinked softly. "You belong . . . somewhere." But I doubted my words as I spoke them. He was spending most of his time here, far too much time to think of himself as "belonging" elsewhere. I eased my hand toward his head and touched him at the base of his ears. In a moment I was scratching his big, firm jowls and stroking him along the muscular arches of his neck and back. His coat was thick and very short. And it was not really grayish brown. I bent closer to part and examine the fur. Each hair, all over his body, was ticked, banded alternately in well defined fawn and dark charcoal. He was marked much like an owl, I marveled, or like the herringbone pattern of some expensive sport coat. I scratched him between his ears; he drew his chin down and arched his neck like a proud little stallion. I smiled and leaned back into a vision of horses whose sleek curves and blowing manes slowly evaporated somewhere up in the blue and gold air.

That evening the big kitty requested to be fed. Over our own dinner Mother, Dad, and I talked about it, and Dad commented that we seemed once again to be acquiring an excess of cats. But he did not really mind.

He smiled, and his dark eyes, a little faded now, crinkled at the corners. Suddenly he yawned, a huge, open yawn like a child would make, and his face turned a gritty gray. This happened a lot now, always toward the ends of meals.

"Dad! Push your chair back! Dad?"

"Yes!" His retort stepped on my question, but his eyes were closed and his right hand was in his plate.

I jerked his chair back, and Mother got his head down to his lap. In about five minutes I was able to help him to the wing chair in the living room. He mumbled, "Big kitty . . . stay . . . nice," and fell into deep sleep.

Mother sat staring inward at the bleakness of her private mindscape. I touched her as I returned to my chair, and my hand noted the knobs and sharp angles of her back and shoulders. We exchanged glances; there was nothing to say that we had not said a hundred times. Dad was still undergoing a series of neurological exams. We tried to finish our dinner and to talk about the new cat.

The big fellow's trust in us bloomed as soon as we put a dish for him out back by the low stone wall, and after that he was never out of sight. In a week or so I introduced him to the carrier, which he accepted with dignity.

The day of his clinic appointment I hefted the carrier onto the front seat of my car, and we rolled down the hill. Quiet and composed he lay on his stomach, his body crowded by the regular size cage.

"You'll be inspected and you'll get your shots," I chattered at him, trying by the fact of my voice to be reassuring. "And as for the neutering," I faltered a moment, "it's for the best, really. Dad has hinted, and rightly, that we do not need to add to the world's surplus of cats." I glanced at him; he was looking at me with diffident and unconcerned attention. I grinned. "What a gentleman you are."

As I brought the car to a stop in the parking lot in front of the Martinez Animal Hospital, I realized the obvious and the embarrassing: we had not given him a name. "Well, whatever am I to tell Bev? She'll need to put a name on your file card in there."

But by the time I had lugged the cage to the reception counter, the perfect designation tingled a little breathlessly on my tongue.

"And what is the kitty's name?" asked Bev, eyeing him with interest after we greeted each other.

"Sir Plus," I answered, standing tall.

Sir Plus brought us a quiet comfort. He never requested entrance into the house, never had a fight with Cinder or Priscilla. The chivalric constancy of his presence was a statement like an arch over a lane leading back to a ranch, or like the granite lions flanking the steps of a public library — something steady and strong, a point of reference. Knowing that he was simply always there and always content was like coming home on a rainy night to lights and laughter and conversation around a hot meal. He was living up to all his name implied.

But after perhaps four months he disappeared, and our disconsolate searches dissolved fruitlessly into the winter's storms and cold. It was not until the first hot day of the next summer that I found him. It was the smell, the awful smell, that led me down the stairs outside from the back toward the lower terrace. At the base of the privet along the west wall, almost where I had first seen him, I saw him now. Or what was left of him. The big body was flattened to a worn scrap. The great domed head lay with the mouth twisted in a mask of agony, and the onyx eyes were gone. From the other side of their gaping sockets a dark maelstrom of emptiness tugged at me; when it sucked me across those dual thresholds I, too, would have no eyes, would rot in the void. I shrank back, acknowledging in a brief shame that the shock of his death was mostly the thud of fear at the base of my skull. Time sucking and pulling. There it was, right in front of me, my own mortality and rush to decay. My nostrils clamped down in denial. I blinked. There were frayed pieces of his ticked fur stuck to his rotting flesh amid the maggots. Clots of busy flies spun like dervishes.

No!

No!

Oh, Sir Plus!

Dad had to throw lime on the remains, and I shoveled them into a plastic garbage bag. We buried the bag.

1988~1990

29

BALANCING

"Paddington, good fellow." I watched his one-eyed approach through the tranquil morning. As a kitten he had lost his left eye to a passing car, and the lids had been stitched closed over the awful hole. He lived next door with John and Ginger Willson, and the sight of his lithe, white form with its big splashes of black always buoyed my spirits. He was coming now to Priscilla and me where we sat on the front porch at the top of the brick steps; from deep inside me a bubble of well-being began wobbling upward. "Good morning."

He answered with a lilting note, and his uncomplicated good will shone from his one round and friendly eye. His presence, like a mug of good coffee, was restorative and companionable.

"And who is this behind you?" I asked as he climbed

the three steps and sat down beside me. I knew that the dark little tabby must be Pearl. John and Ginger had adopted her just days ago after twice rescuing her from high up in one of the massive oaks. Trembling and pleading, she had fled there from her abandonment. She was dainty and feminine, and had a funny double kink at the end of her striped tail. Paddington beamed approval as she came up the steps and onto my lap, and he winked up at me ecstatically. I could almost hear him say, "This is Pearl. I adore her. Isn't she wonderful?"

I smiled from him to her as she made quick little circles in my lap and sank contentedly into her willowy curves. Her easy comfort, her youth, drew me forward into hope and life. This moment, sitting with the cats on the pinkish bricks in a rectangle of sun like lemon butter, was an act of breathing, an interlude in which just to be, to gather back some of the shards of myself. Absently I stroked the velvet dome of Pearl's head and looked at Paddington, so shining and dapper. The blind side of his face was black and gave him a rakish air, as if he were playing pirate. He reached down to give Pearl a lick on her face. There came a stirring of cool air into the warm quiet, and I closed my eyes.

But my anxieties shadowed me everywhere. Everything around me was slipping inexorably through degradation toward its demise. What I accepted intellectually my spirit fought bitterly: everything got old, became diminished and debased. My eyes snapped open, and I glanced at Priscilla. How could she be fourteen years old? I did not want to see the rigid way she sat, or the way her stiff shoulders poked up under the unkempt roughness of her coat. And Mother — thinner and thinner. She ate so little, fell so easily. She never would be strong again. And Dad — an invalid. He had designed this house and built much of it. He literally never was sick. At seventy-nine he still swung his leg over his ten-speed with its thin tires and pedaled over hills for uncounted miles without becoming winded or sore. But now he could not even walk or sit up in bed by himself. Parkinson's Disease: I used to think it happened only to the fundamentally weak, that it just made you stoop and shuffle. Every night I looked in on Dad, then fled to my bathroom and hugged the wall and sobbed. I felt what he was still denying — this was the beginning of the end; his life was over.

And the house — it should be painted, should have a new roof. The furnace — half a century old. The lower lot — it had become a wildly overgrown tangle of twelve foot high pyracantha, blackberry, poison oak, toyons, elderberry. In desperation I had hired a family of husky, golden skinned folk, had taken them down and explained how the growth should be thinned and topped. They had nodded enthusiastically and set to work like delighted demons. At the end of the day when I had returned from work, they were finishing up, and they glowed with pride. But I had gaped in horror; gone was the miniature forest with its meandering, dappled paths and timeless mysteries. Nothing now but mutilated stumps. The west side of the area was denuded, exposed, and the coziness, the winding way down to the graves of the cats, vanished. It would not replenish itself for years, if ever.

Pearl stirred on my lap, pricking my legs. I had quit one of my two part-time jobs and was expanding my private teaching out of my basement office. That way I was almost always where my parents could call to me, where I could stop to do chores, to make arrangements: Meals-On-Wheels. Cleaning. Powers of attorney. Chamber pot buckets under rented commodes. Lesson plans. Yard work. Doctor after doctor. Living trusts. Students. Paying out more than was coming in. "Preneed" arrangements. Ambulances in the middle of the night.

Life had become a frenzied preparation for death. Even after Mother finally, reluctantly, had agreed "to have someone in," and I had hired Yvonne — a wonderful lady who was a dynamo of energy and always upbeat, and who came eight hours a day five days a week — still I was always behind.

What was it all for anyway, this living for dying? What about living for life? Was that only for childhood? Or had it happened when I wasn't looking and therefore not really living?

I set Pearl down, stood, and went to the porch railing to look for Cinder. The changes had troubled her, too. At fourteen she still was fearful of strangers, and the constant comings and goings of people she did not know had driven her out of the house except at night. There was no sign of her now.

I was turning away from the railing to go inside when a movement snagged my attention. A solid little form was trotting up the east side flight of steps. This was Mom Cat, another one belonging to John and Ginger, but this was the first time I had seen her up close. Suddenly

I was chuckling: under a mottled coat like Cinder's, but as if liberally dusted with ashes, Mom Cat's hugely distended belly was swinging from side to side like a leaden pendulum. When she sat down at the top of the stairs, she seemed to inflate, which left her little paws and her delicate face looking ludicrously small. I tried not to laugh. She stared at me. Abruptly she opened to its fullest an astonishingly wide mouth, completely toothless, and ushered out a long sound so pure and strong, so truly and beautifully soprano, as to be worthy of a miniature opera. Amazed, taken aback, I erupted into noisy guffaws. Poor Mom Cat fled in a ponderous waddle back down the stairs.

I opened the door and went inside to begin the day's work. I was still giggling.

30

STILLING

The tires crunched over the summer-hot pavement and pulled the car into a stall at the Martinez Animal Hospital. I turned the key, felt its cool hardness, heard the finality of the click. Insects hummed in the withering air. Temperature gauge, fuel gauge, all the needles sank slowly, and stopped. This was it.

My watch said one fifty. Ten minutes yet. I glanced at Cinder in the carrier beside me and then quickly away and outside. Except for a pickup truck the small lot was empty and quiet. The familiar, low building nestled among its trees. Shaggy junipers, well tended into a grove like craggy cypresses clinging to a sea cliff, enclosed the parking area and made of it a haven, a place of privacy and hope.

Or of partings. I looked at Cinder, at her eyes, those umber agates fixed on the clinic. I saw her sullen, resigned but challenging, guarded, helpless, suspicious. And prescient. Impossible, I supposed, yet I could not tear my gaze from her. Something was going on behind those orbs; she was alive, reacting, feeling, and I saw all that, saw in her eyes the basic pulse of animate life. How could I simply take her in there and . . . Stop it! Get on with life.

But, life was precisely the point. There were times, and now was one of them, when I needed to slip to the side, to honor life by allowing myself to wonder about it, to marvel at it. I looked out the open window toward the domes of the hills. Between them and the clinic, a hundred or so yards away and hidden from my view by the sheltering junipers, people were hurtling past one another at lethal speeds. While they guided the missiles in which they sat, they listened to the radio, they made family plans, personal judgments, professional decisions. But at the base of all that, what allowed all that fantastically complex activity, was essentially the same interaction of electrical impulses and chemicals and atoms of living tissue that impelled the owl in its moth-winged flight across the twilight. The head of state drafting a proposal upon which would pivot the fate of millions, or the spider repairing her web — it was in its essence all the same. This was a thought that for me was always like a burst of light. I could feel it beginning now as a yellow seed, a spiraling bud that lifted and grew and opened in rose and gold, layer from layer and out from my chest and my face. A lotus symphony, it rose bursting and soaring like a sunrise: LIFE. DNA and synaptic leaps. Dust motes and quasars. Such glorious mystery. I could not simply dismiss it in any of its forms.

Cinder. In her cage beside me she was crouched on those slender paws of coal and apricot. Sixteen years ago, as a smudge of challenge and silent determination, she had arrived. Although I had brought her home, it really had been Mother who had rescued her and had loved her always and unconditionally: Cinder swinging from the harness that Mother made for her; Cinder thriving at last on food that Mother cooked for her; Cinder burrowing under Mother's bedspread; Cinder with her leg broken and Mother taking her out on the leash, and Mother lifting her to bed at night and setting her gently down again at daylight; Mother comforting her, calling her "my goody girl" through the time of those dual abscesses and the time of the slit on her belly. And, now, Mother losing everyone: Dad in a nursing home from which he could never return; I conveniently too busy with private students to accompany her along this ultimate and most frightening of paths. Mother's own body was deserting her, evaporating and tossing her in wispy sticks onto the sharpness of her mind and into the void of her loneliness. I fled from that loneliness in cowardice greater than my shame. Her only constant had been her Cinder.

But Cinder had begun to lose weight, and I was mopping up droplets and then small puddles from wherever she sat. With medication and a special diet there had been a brief reprieve in which her tortoiseshell mantle had glowed again, and there were no puddles. Then it began all over, and Dr. Monser said that soon she would begin to suffer. We talked about it, Mother and I, Mother hating it but being practical, and nodding. Then her eyes went flat and dull as if she did not care, and I felt angry and caught and helpless.

And a few minutes ago I had stood in back of her chair near the front door. Cinder was in the carrier, and the carrier was in my hand.

"Mother?"

A silence. *Oh, please.*

"Mother?"

Her answer was her nibbling, her little mouse nibblings at her fingertips. It was a habit I hated because it shouted her loneliness, and I only ran from that and made it worse. She knew. Knew I had Cinder.

"Mother, I must go now." *Oh, help me, please.* I swallowed. "With Cinder. She's here. Do you want to . . . ?"

"Oh, take her and go on!" Closer to the door now, I saw her eyes. They were hard and dry and staring straight at the substitute world contained in a box of color and sound across the room. "I can't look at her. Go on!"

The familiar tide of instant fury — *I was always so angry* — screamed up my throat and this time smashed silently against the knot that blocked me where I swallowed. *Put the cage down.* But, I did not. *Go to her.* I did not. *She's your mother!* I strained toward her. Then I turned with the carrier, stepped out the door, and latched it behind me.

It was one fifty-eight. Another car pulled in, its tires making a gentle shish. A man got out and set down a black puppy with a red leash. The puppy pricked its ears and stumbled off, all eager flops and bounces. A riffle of hot air touched my wet face, and it tugged into a wobbly smile.

I lifted the carrier out of the car and walked with it toward the clinic.

31

LIFTING

Yvonne came scurrying around the corner into the kitchen with Mother's breakfast tray, and skidded to a standstill. Over her glasses she stared at the floor. In a square of sun on the worn linoleum was a great pile of frayed bath towels, clean and haphazardly folded and smelling of cotton hot from the dryer. Beyond their soft mass squatted a white metal tub like a boat, and next to it an enameled cup holding a tall plastic bottle. Beyond all that there I was, in old jeans and a tee shirt, seated on the floor like an attenuated Buddha. Steam rose from a deep pan of water on the stove.

"Well!" She grinned. "Do you think you're ready?"

"No."

Our laughter lightened the kitchen. I stood up and looked reluctantly at the breakfast tray as Yvonne placed it on the drainboard. A heaviness settled on me, and Yvonne's mouth fell at the corners. Coffee barely sipped. The egg had only two tiny triangles cut from it, and of the two strips of bacon only one had been nibbled. A small piece of toast, buttered and spread with currant jelly, lay untouched. I could hear Mother's doctor say once again, "If it doesn't bite you back, eat it!" Anything! She needed calories, actually needed fat. But thin and shrunken even before the fall that months ago had shattered her right knee, she no longer had the strength to rise from her bed upstairs. Upstairs because the more shadowed light was easier on her eyes. I sucked in my breath and wrenched around. It was wrong to turn away from that tray, and hopeless to confront it. My glance slid across Yvonne's sobered expression, and I headed for the basement while she cleared the tray and washed the few dishes.

The trick, I thought as I trotted down the stairs, was to put on blinders, to focus. To focus on this hot, clear day with the buckeye trees already wearing the crinkled copper of their autumn cycle. To focus on the air beginning to deepen to a light gold, turning the landscapes into Claude Lorrain paintings. To focus on this day of no students. And on this afternoon when Earl and I would go to a movie and to an early dinner. For a while I would be in the midst of movement and sound and things ahead and hope. Earl. The ring, the "going steady" ring with the single, blue-green zircon, was always a new feeling on my finger. Its quiet elegance had graced others during generations in his family. "My mother said you might like this," he had offered as I opened the little box.

I felt a sudden easing, as in a stirring of cool air on

hot skin. I stepped into my office, where Priscilla lay stretched out on her pad in front of the glowing coils of the little heater. With Cinder gone Priscilla had spent last winter's nights inside. She slept either on my lap with her head in the crook of my arm, or as close to the heater as she could get without singeing her wool. Now even through the summer she had sought the penetrating heat. I watched her a while, reluctant to rush Yvonne or to wake the old kitty.

What were we getting into with this bath idea? Neither Priscilla nor I, nor Yvonne, had any experience with the event, and although Priscilla no longer was claustrophobic in the house, I never confined her against her will. I shook my head; yesterday I had lifted her carefully, thinking to try placing her in one side of the divided kitchen sink, which would make a convenient tub. Before her feet were even near the top of that waterless pool, she had begun to twist her brittle body and to yowl. No matter how many of her legs I gathered up, she always had at least three more whose paws pushed frantically away from the sink in front, in back, to the side. But, she was so dirty! The towel on her pad was clean yesterday, and today it would have to go in the wash.

I sat on the floor beside her and stroked her sleeping form. She had spent the summer following me around inside and outside, squinting and blinking, hoping to be taken up and carried. She still had moments of, rather stiffly, chasing a leaf or starting to dash up the birch by the lawn. She would still tap me on my ankle, and bark to get my attention. She stayed with me when I watered the vinca minor along the upper road. When the sun was warmest on the driveway gravel, she snoozed there on her back with her legs loosely apart.

The most obvious sign of her vulnerability was that she no longer groomed herself. Along her hind legs, at her flanks, and by her elbows, hung clots of fur. I had tried brushing her coat, but the brush would not penetrate its thickness, and a comb's gentle tugs caused her pain. I tried cutting off the clumps, but they seemed full of nerve fibers where they swung from her skin, and she could not abide the parting. *Mother, lying on her back upstairs on her bed, naked and spread-eagled because she could not abide the touch of even a sheet.* At last I had used a dampened sponge, and daily I took Priscilla on my lap to gently sponge her down. The sponge would come away soiled after every stroke, and I would squeeze it out in the pan of warm water, and stroke again. Then I would towel her off, and she would look a little better. But still the fleas hid at the base of her tail, and her white looked — and smelled — like congealed mutton grease against her scrambled egg yellow. So today was our day, Yvonne's and mine, to give her a real bath, a bath with lots of warm water and feline shampoo. Yvonne had made Mother as comfortable as possible, and Priscilla had finished a big breakfast some time ago. *"There," Mother would say, "I've done quite well." I would look, dismayed, from her nearly untouched plate to her hollow cheeks, her washboard chest, her thighs no thicker than a girl's arms.* I blinked away the vision, turned off the heater, and reached for Priscilla.

She was cradled comfortably in my arms until we emerged into the kitchen. Then her head came up instantly, her body stiff, her nose quivering. All that strange stuff on the floor! She began to wiggle. Yvonne closed all the doors as I lowered Priscilla slowly into the empty oval tub. It was shallow enough that she could see out, and wide enough that she could not easily grab its chipped rim.

"Easy, Priscilla girl." Her claws scrabbled on the enameled bottom, and her back humped and bucked. My left hand had her firmly by the nape of her neck. With the first pouring of warm water she yowled with the outrage that sparked from her eyes.

"Look at that!" Yvonne exclaimed. "The water just rolls right off of her."

I nodded. Darned fur. Like plunging your hand into the fleece on a sheep's back. "Pour fast. We've got to get down to her skin. And we've got to do this whole thing quickly, so she doesn't get cold."

Ten cupsful later of warm water, a glowering Priscilla was wet through and was scrambling for the rim of the tub. She showered us and the cabinet fronts. Choppy wavelets of dingy water crested the tub and slopped the floor. Locked on her nape, my left hand ached already. A stale, wet wool smell wrapped around us.

"Yuck."

Yvonne grinned and poured the clear, yellow shampoo over Priscilla from neck to end of tail. Three hands massaged her while she thrashed and splashed and sent up an endless, piercing wail that hurt my ears. A blob of gray suds flew up and smacked Yvonne on her glasses. She reared back, dripping and sputtering with surprised laughter. The water in the tub was black, and Priscilla looked as if we had just fished her from the sewer. Brown-black water ran from my arms and blotched my shirt.

"We've got to suds her again," I shouted over her howl. I scooped her out of the tub and pressed her against me into the towel that Yvonne had stuffed between us. She nodded, and as she emptied the tub into the sink, I felt a thin sheet of sudsy wet run down my chest and sides into my waist band and onto my groin. The soaked towel slid like a dumpling to my lap. Yvonne whisked the empty tub back to the floor and, glasses off, she crouched above us with the cup. In silence she poured fresh, warm water. We scrubbed, and quickly there boiled up a white froth like meringue. Priscilla suddenly gave up the physical fight, and glared straight ahead in a pout punctuated by a loud, grumpy whine. A strong odor of fake lemon assailed us from the foam. We looked at each other.

"Whew!"

We giggled as Yvonne emptied the tub again. But as we began to rinse with warm water, and my left wrist began to cramp, Priscilla started to shiver. Her eyes emptied of their vital anger and showed only dull resignation. A needle of alarm pricked my throat.

"Pour it on fast, Yvonne. We've got to get her out of here."

She nodded and poured and massaged and poured. How unsubstantial, how naked and flat, Priscilla seemed with her saturated fur pasted to the knobs of her little frame. Nothing to her. *I stood by the bed. Mother was sitting up, unclothed, washed in a shaft of afternoon sun through the dormer. She was studying her upraised hand, the straight fingers fanned slightly apart. In her eyes a dawning realization struggled with denial. "Look! You can see right through my hand!" I knew. I looked. I saw an X ray.*

The warm light passed through the lifted palm and out the back of the hand in a glow of flesh pink. It outlined each bone, each little flare of joint, from the tips of her fingers to her wrist. Slowly she lay back down. "I can't live like this!" My gaze slipped to her abdomen — the pale skin lay like moist dough over a topography of coils — and back to her eyes. Sadness, fear-tinged resignation . . .

Abruptly I lifted Priscilla from the tub and into the folds of a dry towel. Almost instantly the water soaked it to a sodden lump that slid to the floor. Yvonne handed me another, and hurried the remaining ones down to reheat them in the dryer. While she was gone, I enveloped Priscilla in the fluffy cloth and patted and blotted and gently rubbed. She looked at me, bleak and forlorn. I looked back, and the world fell away in a cold wind. She dissolved in a blur.

"Oh, Priscilla kitty, I'm so sorry, so awfully sorry." I looked around the kitchen at the faded walls and into a jumble of images of Mother and Dad. I looked back at Priscilla. I rocked and rubbed and rocked and consoled her, and felt her shiver. She burrowed her head against my body. We clung to each other there on the puddled floor with my jeans dark with cold water and my shirt clammy on my skin. I shivered in my own cold. Yvonne's quick steps up the stairs brought the hot, dry towels. We folded the groggy kitty into their warmth, and slowly, as I rocked and massaged and comforted her, her shivering ebbed, and finally stopped. She was asleep. I peeled the towel back from her shoulders. The fur was springy and damp and redolent with "Citrus Scent."

I carried her back down to my office, where Yvonne had turned the little heater back on and placed the pad nearby. I spread the last dry towel on the pad, and laid the sleeping Priscilla down. Her coat was beginning to fluff, and there was a shine to the drying hairs. Some of the tangles and knots had opened slightly, and I went to work with comb and scissors. When she was totally dry and awake, there would be a special treat of warm, moist cat food all wonderfully gloppy and stinky.

Yvonne padded down and peeked in. I gave her a thumbs up sign, and her face lifted in a happy grin.

1992~1993

32

DECISION

He came head down, the left foreleg held against his chest, the right showing a ragged gash of red along its inner length. He hobbled up the porch steps, and sank into himself a little ways from Priscilla and almost on top of Earl's feet. This was the worst yet. Earl tilted his head; like a naughty child I tensed against what I knew was coming: "You've either got to adopt him or have him put down."

I stared at that huddle of gray at our feet. I scanned the unkempt coat, too finely thin for January, and all those shiny ticks poking their swollen rears through the patchy fur. How much blood were they sucking from him?

"Are you feeding him anything? He's dropped a lot of weight."

I scowled. Suddenly the cat sneezed several times, his white forepaws lifting right off the bricks.

"Oh, why can't he just go home?"

"I think," Earl said, "that he's telling you some-thing."

I watched Earl down the walk, and felt my face tighten. Yes, but I did not want to hear that something. I did not want another anything just now, and especially not another being — not even another cat — to whom to give my heart, and to care for, and to watch die. I glanced at Priscilla as she sat on the cold bricks observing the stray. I must get her inside, sponge and comb her, and set out her pad by the heater. I breathed in on a shiver and glanced up at the little coin of sun so remote and shrunken. Old sun, faded to silver like my father's eyes in his skull face. My glance slid down across Priscilla's stiffness, across the jowly stray with his runny nose, and I fled indoors to the kitchen. I gave the burner a vicious twist into life under the coffee water. Old, old, old! Everything, everybody old! And in the end . . . Mother was gone a year now, but the specter of her going still clung about me like a wet sheet. If only I could pare everything down to a clean new core, a beginning, everything young, strong, vital, and thrusting forward.

Still shivery I sat with my hands clenched and tingling around my hot mug. That cat out there — he must belong to someone. When I first saw him two or three weeks ago out by the garage, he had been skittering along in a crouch, just a big-headed sausage of gray and white. I had called, "Kitty, kitty?" and he had stopped. His small, slanted eyes had been wary, but as I asked him

about himself he had relaxed and sat down. Another tom
on a prowl, I had thought, and forgot about him. But a
morning or two later there he was on the porch, where he
and Priscilla sat amicably regarding each other.

His visits increased until I was seeing him every day
several times a day. I fed him nothing, but I enjoyed
chatting with him and trying to fathom his personality.
His eyes, like a kitten's always brimming with wonder
and questions, were set in a warrior's face with careless
smudges of charcoal high on either side of his nose.
His ears seemed extra wide apart, and their tips were
serrated and worn like a pair of badlands' buttes. And
those jowls! He had a way of approaching my feet as if
he were about to attack them. Was this a game, or did he
mean it? It was unnerving, and I would not touch him.
Yet he treated Priscilla with friendly respect. He made
me smile, and he made me uneasy.

Each day saw him thinner and more ragged. I had
telephoned Animal Control, had searched telephone
poles for flyers, had asked Ginger and John. No leads
anywhere. Then came the limping and the swelling ticks.
Yesterday the whitish third eyelids were half way across
his eyes. Now, this morning, that bloody gash on his
foreleg . . .

I sighed; I knew all along what I must do. Leaving
my coffee, I fetched the carrier and some of Priscilla's
pellets. Out on the porch I set the feed on the floor of
the cage, and fastened its door open. Before I could lift
Priscilla to take her indoors, the stray was half in the
carrier and crunching the pellets in starved gulps. The
carrier became his refuge, and a few mornings later I

fastened the door on him and took him to the Martinez Animal Hospital.

"The kitty's name?" Bev inquired.

"No," I wagged my head at her over the reception counter, "no name, not yet. Let's see if he's salvageable."

She nodded, and in a moment the cat and I were alone in one of the small examination rooms. The quiet gloom, the steel table, and above it the unlit eye of the big lamp, chilled me. I pressed my moist palms to the warm insides of my jacket pockets. On the snick of the door latch my breath snagged and held, and Dr. Monser, entering, flipped on the light. His eyebrows bristled into arcs when he tipped the cat out of the carrier and fixed his glance on the forelegs.

"What a hulk!"

Startled, I looked, and for the first time I saw beyond the blood and the torn, white fur. The veterinarian was smoothing the hair over a shape that from paw to elbow was exactly the contour of a man's well-muscled forearm, the graceful dip at the wrist swelling into firmly curved and rounded cords above. My breath eased out as the doctor and I grinned at each other.

All through that day of students I rode on the ridiculous lift occasioned by Dr. Monser's remark. It was not until I was returning to the clinic that I began again to swallow around the possibilities of feline leukemia, feline AIDS, or who knew what sort of fever brought on by those ticks. I could not imagine that the agreed upon neutering could be done yet. As I waited in the examination room, I thought about feeding the cat on the porch, and getting properly acquainted, and . . . my glance flew to the opening door. In Dr. Monser's arms was a sleepily befuddled gray and white cat, limp and warmly mussed from drugged slumber. The veterinarian placed him on the table.

"He's fine," he smiled. "Temperature normal, no diseases, just a bit of battle fatigue. I gave him his inoculations."

"He's neutered, too?"

"Yes. And while I was at it I cleaned up his legs and got rid of those ticks. I also removed this from under the skin at the base of his tail." He placed in my palm something gray and irregular, hard and cold, the size of a large pea. "Somebody's been using him for target practice."

I looked from Dr. Monser to the rag-doll cat with his wobbling head and unfocused, dilated pupils. Target practice! Out at the counter I groped through an angry haze. A gun was being raised, leveled, . . .

". . . and," Bev was finishing, "you need to keep the kitty inside for the next four days."

Inside! I had not considered that. This creature which I had not even touched was to share my living space? For four days?

Out in the parking lot, while a freezing mist gusted over the car and beaded the windows, I sat for a moment and stared at the carrier on the seat beside me. "Well! Well, well."

And we started for home.

33

ONE MORE

In the ten minute drive home from the clinic
the wan afternoon faded into darkness, and along the
road headlight reflections dropped down abysses of wet
shine. I turned up the car's heater. The tires shisshed,
and I wondered where, where, could I put this cat for the
required four days. "Certainly not in the house," I said
to the carrier as we rolled into the driveway. "Not yet.
Not fair to Priscilla; it's her house now."

I turned off the motor. The warm car was a friendly
cave; I snuggled deeper into the seat and gazed distractedly
at the white glare of my headlights on the garage. I held
up the pellet which Dr. Monser had placed in my hand.
In the gloom its hard shape was like the silhouette of some
distant boulder. I closed my fist over it, smacked my hand
into my lap, and turned to the carrier. "Have you ever

been indoors?" Silence. A vision of shattered porcelain, of a panicked streak of gray and white . . . I shook my head and turned back to the reflected light in front of us. The garage, could it be "indoors" for four days?

I left the carrier on the car seat and hunched through the mist into the garage. I flipped on the single bulb, and stood shaking with cold in the thin light. A draft of wet air was leaching around the edges of the north window and drifting across the expanse of concrete floor. It smelled of dankness and metal, and it sucked the warmth from my clothes. In one corner were a few lengths of old two-by-fours and some empty cardboard cartons. I set to work.

On the first of several trips between the house and the garage I brought out a space heater, plugged it in, and watched its coils turn a cheerful vermilion. I dragged the two-by-fours over, knocked the cardboard cartons flat, and laid them across the timbers. Another trip for a load of old bath towels and a scarred wooden chair. More trips. Soon I had a water bowl, a food dish, a litter tray, and a small oval rug destined for the dump. Closer than prudent to the glow from the heater I stood panting and clammy in the middle of the clutter. My teeth were clicking. My feet did not feel quite connected to the concrete. I folded layers of towels onto the flattened cartons over the timbers where I would set the carrier. Next, the old rug went down on the cement between the carrier pad and the old chair. I lined up the bowls to one side. There. A cozy and tidy living room. But suddenly it seemed to tilt and, when I swallowed, my throat puckered and crawled. I fetched the carrier, placed it on the towels with its door open, and I wobbled away into the house.

After hot soup and a nap, and layered in flannel and down, I returned to the garage with a small offering of food. From the open carrier the cat's eyes, the pupils still dilated, surveyed his surroundings. "Hello, there." It was a whisper around the rawness in my throat. Not quite returned from far away, he blinked up at me, and half tumbled in slow motion from the carrier to the platform to the rug. The heater had pushed back the dampness a little, and I sat close to watch the cat reconnect himself. He was like a kitten just learning to engage his rear quarters; as his front end moved forward, his hind legs tottered sideways, and his tail flopped. He lapped a little water and found the food, but the litter tray was still beyond his awareness. I lifted him and placed him on the sand. His hind end sat down and brought the rest of him with it; in the feeble scramble to right himself he got to pawing the litter. It registered; he lowered his head to investigate, bumped his nose, and sneezed. I picked him up and sank onto the chair where the heat could flow around us. Blessed heat. Heat over my legs, heat from the supine form on my lap, heat creeping up and out to my hands on the cool fur. How fine it was, a promise of silken plush, like rabbit hair. My muscles began to ease. My fingers stroked . . . soft fur . . . legs getting warm . . . floating . . .

My head snapped down and my eyes opened to meet those of the cat, his more focused now and regarding my face. "Mmrrmm?" he asked, his mouth closed and his body pumping once like a bellows. Smiling and swallowing over the feel of ashes in my throat, I unplugged the heater for the night. Another "Mmrrmm?" reached me as I clicked off the light and closed the door.

The next morning, with a fever lifting me in waves of lightheadedness, I took some kibble to the garage, and my new charge came trotting to me across the old rug. He was moving normally now, and was hungry. He gobbled his breakfast before I could even plug in the heater and sit down. Carefully I set him on my lap, and he looked down, ears pricked, at the heater coils whanging into warmth and color. Poor ears, like thin chamois rimmed with old notches and tears, a chronicle of his days. His eyes were a clear, shallow green, almond shaped, ordinary but for their look of unguarded innocence. What would I call him? "Pandora." Hardly. "Flannel." Perhaps; that was homely, honest, soft. Names came and I tried saying them aloud, but my voice cracked or cut out, and my throat was tight and hard.

I squeaked and jerked back. The cat had changed position on my lap such that he was facing my chest, the movement completed with no warning, no graceful uncoiling or sinuous flow, just a flop as swift as an attack. He fixed me with another "Mmrrm." All of him abruptly, unexpectedly, expanded and subsided when he spoke. My breath sputtered in a giggle. I stayed with him until we were both warm, then I unplugged the heater and left.

This set the pattern and the tone of my visits. I came out every couple of hours, always with a little food, always plugging in the heater when I entered and unplugging it when I left, always staying for a chat and some lap time. I made certain to pet Priscilla before I went to the garage and again when I returned, in the hope of getting them more accustomed to each other's scent. He began running to the garage door as soon as he heard me on the porch, his eager cries coming dimly through the wood. I had, indeed, one more cat.

Sunday my voice was only a croak, and between each chore I had to lie down. I canceled my Monday students and called Earl while I could still whisper. In the garage the cat waited for me to plug in the heater and then jumped to my lap, his white belly-bellows pumping his murmurs. "Claude." No. It was an appropriately short, stocky name, but too formal, too ceremonious. "Finnegan." Maybe.

The next day I awoke knowing what the cat's name would be, and I opened my mouth to try the sound of it. Nothing happened. Not even a breathy whisper. I did chores, tended to Priscilla, and made my visits to the garage. I drank endless cups of lemon tea, but my throat was like a cold stone.

In the late afternoon Earl appeared with a great cauldron of his homemade vegetable soup, and its aroma through the house was like a benediction. I set the table with bread and fruit, grabbed a pad of paper, and soon we sat down in the warm kitchen to a light, hot supper. Earl talked. I bobbed my head and scribbled. When he asked if I had settled on a name yet for the stray, I nodded and wrote, and shoved the pad to him.

" 'Juan Mo Cat,' " he read aloud as if translating. His brow puckered.

I took the pad, wrote, and pushed it across the table again.

" 'One more cat,' " he pronounced with deliberation. "'He's just Juan Mo Cat. 'Mo' for short.' " Earl's eyes began to sparkle, and his moustache pulled up at the corners. The kitchen filled with his gentle laughter.

34

MO

Thippity–thippitythippitythippity– WHUMP.

"Mo! You okay?"

He shook himself, and rocketed on up to the top. What was this constant falling up the stairs? I followed now two at a time, but he was already under my bed. From beneath the flounce his forelegs stuck out, paws spread, as he patted the carpet and began the tag-the-moving-shoe game. Now and then his head came into view upside down with his eyes sparkling, and the room was lighter and sunnier than it had been for a long time.

When I finished the bed, he thumped back downstairs in a rush to the front door. There were new spring grasses to walk among and to sniff, and his special friend Redman would be somewhere in the yard. I would not be Mo's jailer. But my gaze followed him as he trotted off; what I saw were the times he tried the jump from the kitchen floor to the sink and fell back on his side without managing more than half the distance.

So this first year with Mo was turning into one of discoveries. Already, in just three months, he had gone through one prescription of antibiotics for an upper respiratory infection, and half a prescription of Prednisolone for respiratory allergies. The little cabinet in the basement hallway had a drawer filling with his toys and his medications.

His personality opened layer upon layer. Inside the house he followed me everywhere, clinging to my legs with his busy-busy Shetland pony trot: back and forth in the kitchen, from kitchen to living room, from there to upstairs and down again. If I closed him out of the bathroom, he meowed and pawed at the door, and I felt guilty of inexcusable rejection. He followed Priscilla, also. She was too fragile now for play, but Mo tagged along behind her with his chest against her tail and his head to one side. When he tapped her haunch in an invitation to play, she would give a little bark of pain; with his eyes full of questions he would watch her hobble away. She slept a great deal, and often Mo would curl around her, murmuring, to wash her face and ears.

At night he usually slept on top of my bed upstairs, and he was often ready to retire before I finished my bedtime coffee in the kitchen. He would be sitting, watching me, and then he would get up abruptly — all his movements were abrupt, never any transition or flow — and trot-trot to the loosely latched door of the downstairs bedroom. Up would go a paw, and he would pound the door, socking it on every bounce: Bangety-bangety-bang!

"Mo!"

Two or three seconds of silence. Then: Bangety-BANG!

"Mo!!"

"Meeaaow!"

He had strong opinions, too, about being asked to get down from my office chair. I would whisper his name to wake him. He would chirp a sleepy question that turned to petulance the instant he perceived my intention.

"May I, Mo?"

He would set his teeth on my arm in warning. I would scoop him up all in one motion which forced his breath and his annoyance out together in a surprised squeak. His pout forgotten, he would relax against my chest for a cuddle.

With a quick thudding of paws he was usually the first one down to my office when private students arrived. He sampled laps, and then curled up on mine, his chin resting heavily on the hard table edge as he drifted down into sleep. Soon, when only his white muzzle and pink nose were visible, the students would nudge one another and point and grin.

Why, then, with all his obvious love of companionship, did I not foresee what he would do that June morning? After a week of house confinement and pills to quell a bout of his heavy sneezing and wheezing, he and Priscilla had breakfast on the front porch in the bluish cool of its shade. The white sun was just up. I set out jogging on the upper road and feeling the early freshness take me out of myself. I thudded back down, past my house, through the silent air that filled suddenly with mockingbird song. Tossed like water from a Spanish fountain, the music hung a moment, then spilled down over me and into the winking grasses. A half mile into this world, I turned — and stopped. What the . . . ? That squat, gray body with the thin, horizontal tail. That white front. Mo. About thirty feet away, he came trotting toward me, looking determined. His chest was so broad that his elbows stuck out. His rather dainty forefeet were pronated as they padded over the pavement. I jogged back to the pepper tree at the foot of my hill with Mo right behind me. I went on along the lower road. I passed the curve where long ago Dad had picked up Tarik's warm body, and then past the stone wall where even longer ago I had found Tai. I stopped. Mo had followed me at a fast trot for nearly a mile. He sat down, raised a paw, and tapped my leg. I lifted him against my chest. "You little fool," I whispered. He touched his nose to mine. I swallowed and, holding him, I jogged all the way back to the house. He, at least, had had plenty of exercise; his heart was thudding against my hand.

John and Ginger gave Mo carte blanche visiting rights. If I missed him at home I was likely to find him in their patio with Redman or Big Guy or Pearl, or coming out their back door after a visit and a snack.

Earl was away in November, and the Willsons invited me for Thanksgiving dinner whenever I returned from being with Dad in the nursing home. At dusk, searching for the part of myself that was always ripped away in those visits, I fed Priscilla inside and Mo on the porch. Through a light rain I walked next door. There were about five of us in the warmth and cheer and savory aromas of the big kitchen. In a few minutes we heard a scratching at the door. Ginger opened it, and in came Mo. When we all sat down at the oval table in the dining room to a feast of turkey, salads, stuffing, potatoes, cranberry relish, and pies, John took Mo up and put him on his lap at the head of the table. This was, after all, an Occasion. Mo sat, regal in his place of honor. His eyes got bigger and bigger, and his nostrils worked in pulsing lifts as John hand fed him bits of turkey. We all watched with indulgent grins while we chatted about food and Christmas and possible sales at Mervyn's and Nordstrom's.

Much later Mo and I walked back home. We both were smiling.

35

MOVING ON

Priscilla wobbled on the dirt border between the escallonia and the lawn, where I was doing the morning watering. This summer, more than other summers, she stayed right beside me. It was hard for her; it meant climbing steps from the lower to the upper terrace, keeping out of the way of cars on the upper road, and always, always, seeking stillness and sun. Now, with the spray from the hose drifting against her, wet and too cool, she moved away.

It hurt me to watch her. She was eighteen now, and her years had settled her neck into a frozen arch, so that she looked more and more like old Socrates in his last weeks. The past few days her normally good appetite had withered, and this morning she had just blinked at her food. With a wrench I realized that she looked shriveled and wispy, and I was suddenly in Mother's upstairs bedroom again: *"Look, Sandra. You can see right through my hand!"*

Mo erupted from behind us with his ears up and his tail curved over his back. He slapped Priscilla on her fanny. She tottered, gave a little cry, and limped away. Wistful, Mo sat down and gazed after her.

By the time I finished the yard chores it was hot, Mo had melted into the shade, and I lifted Priscilla to take her inside where I could watch her. I held her on my lap to sponge and comb her. She nuzzled under my arm and fell asleep. She smelled stale, the way she had smelled the time she was so terribly ill. Was this going to be the end? Another thread ready to snap?

My afternoon students finished by four o'clock, and I went up to water the vinca minor along the upper road. Priscilla was by my feet. But where were her yips, her ankle taps, her squints and blinks? A cardboard cutout, she leaned against my leg. I stood holding the hose, thankful to feel the hard thrust of the water through it, to lose myself in the rainbows that formed and unformed across the rushing arch of drops. There was a slight smell of tar, and the pavement steamed where the water hit it. Priscilla had fallen asleep against my shoe; her coat was plastered with wetness like grease on a fried egg. I lifted her to her feet, then moved to adjust the hose. When I turned back, she was in the sun in the middle of the road, asleep flat on her side. At the sound of an approaching car I scooped her up, and she did not even open her eyes. The hose forgotten, I held her, and walked and walked with her in the sun.

I talked to her. I postponed the telephone call I knew I must make.

Dr. Monser's gaze fell on Priscilla's roached back as she huddled against me on the table. In the nearly eighteen hours since I had called, she had eaten nothing, had drunk nothing. My throat cramped as I felt her head burrow under my elbow. I curved my free arm around her, my skin against her faded wool. "I think she's dying."

Gently the veterinarian pulled her away and palpated her kidneys. He shook his head and frowned. I bit my upper lip. He opened her mouth wide, and lowered his face to hers. He sniffed once, then twice. "I smell urine."

I stared at him.

"It's very strong." His voice softened. "You are right; she's dying. Her kidneys are in failure."

I blinked. "There's no help?"

"No. She might live another day."

Priscilla leaned against me again, her head under my arm. But the table was gone, and a darkness tugged at her, pulling her away, pulling at memories of sunny mornings and the sharp scent of eucalyptus.

"Is she suffering?"

"Yes."

I looked at her. If I moved, she would topple. *Oh, God. How could I tell Dad?* I tried to smile, to put off the finality. "Look at her. Hiding from the bad things."

He nodded. And waited.

"You'd best put her to sleep now."

He took her from me. My sudden tears were so thick a film that she was instantly converted to a blurred memory. A box of tissues materialized, and I was alone in the quiet of the little room.

I drove home slowly by a back way, slowly in order to listen to the high-pitched buzz of summer insects and to smell the hot dust on the roadside weeds. The air cooled my wet face. To leave a death behind, even a small death, seemed to me an act of treason, an ultimate and unpardonable abandonment. But without the turning away, how could I move forward? How could I move forward without remorse? That, I suddenly realized, was what human funeral and memorial services were about. They were a way to mill around a bit, to gather essences within the comfort of familiar voices. A pause at an oasis. A rite of passage. But I had grown up in a family who did not observe such rites or the special significance of certain days: no birthday celebrations, no Mother's Days or Father's Days, no graduation parties, no obituaries or services. Nothing to promote a selfish center of attention. Nothing, I saw now, to serve as markers — "This is where I have been" — along the miles.

I looked up and away to the hills, to their black-green oaks and the sweeps of yellow-bright grasses about the same color as Priscilla's coat in her youth. I saw her and Prudence as babies with Mother feeding them in the loft of the red barn. The thick, green leaves of the alfalfa bales had smelled and tasted like tea. Down the hill I saw Dad as we scrubbed up the old hen house.

The tires crunched over the gravel in my driveway. The bottom part of the camellia bush by the dining room quivered, and out burst Mo. Trot-trot-busy-busy up onto the porch. "Mmrrrmm?" A single pumping — air in, air out.

I smiled. Tomorrow when I visited Dad and he asked me about Priscilla, I somehow would tell him. And I would tell him, too, more about Mo. He had never met Mo, but he knew he carried a bellows low in his belly.

36

STRUGGLES

From ground to trunk and back again, Mo and Pearl tagged each other, claws snicking across the bark of the Willsons' redwood tree. From my porch I watched while the fresh morning rode up the breeze off the straits. Newly washed, Mo's comb rested in my hand.

Without Priscilla for a companion, Mo was spending more and more of the remaining summer with the Willsons' cats. In the drowsy times he and shy Redman relaxed together, their eyes half-closed. In the cool of the mornings and evenings, Mo and Pearl romped and tumbled over each other. Sometimes he stayed so late at night that I put the comb away on its shelf without his coming home at all. I missed his presence on the bed then, and I was always anxious on the way to the door in the mornings. But there he would be on the mat, his front paws tucked under his white vest, waiting for his breakfast.

Then one morning he was not there. I called and waited. I searched. I told myself that he would be along. The kitchen clock tugged the hours up and over its arc until at last it was evening. Ginger called to ask why Mo had not been over.

He returned the next afternoon, but there was something about the set of his body, a slight tightness, that was not right. He climbed, rather than stepped, into the house. Without a glance at his favorite kitchen chair he curled up on a corner of the dining room rug, and he slept there most of the afternoon and evening. Just before bedtime he came sneezing around to the couch and put his front paws up on the seat. He crouched. He made push-off motions. Then he gave it up, his gaze abstracted in the focus of pain.

"Mo, what's wrong?" I lifted him as if he were a fragile petal, but he squeaked in a burst of hurt and settled himself fretfully against the cushions. I stayed to run my fingers between his ears and down his neck, over and over, until at last he eased into sleep.

At eleven thirty the next morning I set him on the table at the clinic. Dr. Monser examined the claws, spreading them apart under the light, feeling their tips. His forehead puckered as he looked across at me. "He's been hit by a car, a glancing blow that skated him right across the pavement." He showed me the split, frayed nails. "Nothing else would do that. He's lucky, but also extremely sore. Keep him in about a week." His eyebrows plunged as Mo sneezed again. "And let's get him back on the Prednisolone."

The allergies responded immediately. The body soreness evolved into pain that over the next five days bore down on Mo and gathered itself into his lower chest and his left hind leg. He cried as if he were being stabbed. He limped slowly after me from room to room. The stairs were the worst; they took him agonizing minutes, but he would not permit me to lift him. If I closed him into the kitchen, he wailed like a Siamese and banged an endless, lonely rhythm on the door. In another day he was reluctant to walk at all, and stood about with his back roached and the offending leg held such that the toes barely reached the floor. Before lying down he would circle and recircle and circle again, three legged, and I could see in his eyes that his entire being was snared on his distress.

One evening I made my sleep camp in the bedroom off the kitchen so that he would not be so alone at night. But as soon as I climbed into bed and the room was dark, he came hobbling with small, hopeful cries to stand just below my head. He tried to drag himself up the covers. Somehow I got him onto the bed. He slept long past the sunrise over Mount Diablo.

Before noon we were back in the hospital, this time for full-body X rays. A pellet like that other one, in his thorax about half an inch below and to the right of his spine, snatched my breath, but it was old and best left alone. Dr. Monser pointed to a crack in the sternum, probably new. There was a crack or separation where the left hip joined the pelvis, and there was some loss there of the necessary vertebrae space for the sciatic nerve. The bony structures were closing down around the nerve like teeth.

"If the pinching progresses, the pain will prevent bowel movements. Watch him for signs of constipation." The doctor looked hard at the floor. "The worst case scenario," he continued, his gaze finding mine again, "is paralysis of the hind legs."

But thoughts of the future evaporated in the immediacy of the next minutes there on the table. Dr. Monser called in two assistants, and asked that I stand away. It was important to know Mo's temperature; if it was elevated, that would be an indication of probable infection in the cracked bones. But temperatures were taken rectally, and because of the hip injury the full insertion of the thermometer was excruciating. Mo exploded from his lethargy with a screech, twisted into a blur, and slashed and bit at three pairs of restraining hands. His eyes blazed with his desperation. I flinched from his screams and rubbed my clammy palms on my shirt. A muzzle mask appeared, and in a moment Mo looked like some creature that never was — a furry, struggling body with a head like a dead pig's. Quickly then a cortisone injection in that rear leg, one of antibiotics into his nape, and the removal of the thermometer. It was over. The muzzle was off. Mo was back in his cage.

At home Ginger brought over a big carrier like a kennel crate, spacious and airy, and I set it up under the kitchen table. Following Dr. Monser's instructions I put the litter tray up against one side of the crate, the water and food dishes up against the other. Mo was to be confined to this tiny space. There was to be an absolute minimum of walking, no stairs, no being lifted, no access to any other part of the house. I tried to forget how often I had lifted him, tried to shut out the images of his crawling upward on stairs that had become mountains while I cheered him on, thinking that he must exercise sore muscles. What had I done to him? But his temperature was normal, and that gave me hope. Time and that injection of cortisone were the boosters that might help his body heal itself.

The days dragged into a week and then into a second week. Mo's only interest was sleeping, and I draped a towel over his crate to mute the light. It seemed that whenever I approached him it was with an antibiotic pill, but he took them with no more protest than the raising of a foreleg. He slept and drank and slept and ate. I was elated to find that I needed to scoop his litter box.

Another ten days ticked past. Like a slow dawn, the light began to return through his eyes, and they shone with interest in the doings around him. A few mornings later he came out of the crate without that tense arch to his back. His left rear foot rested comfortably on the floor. A silent cheer rushed up through my throat, and I knew then how long I had been holding my breath.

We celebrated. I got out his blue comb, and there on the floor under the table I combed him for a long time. He relaxed and purred, and exhibited the first sense of general well-being in nearly a month. He fell asleep on his side against my leg, his head back and my fingers stroking his white chin and throat. How extraordinarily wide was the space between the backs of his jaws.

The kitchen clock ticked a counterpoint into the rectangles of sun on the cool floor. I closed my eyes. Suddenly, through the screen door flooded a mockingbird's song. In all the world there was no better place at that moment than right there under my kitchen table with my cat, who was going to heal and be whole again.

37

ACCEPTING

I first glimpsed him as a small halo flitting along the pale stucco of the Willsons' walls. The sun was up but not yet flaring among the branches of the sprawling valley oak that sheltered their house; in their flagstoned courtyard I stood and rattled the kibble. The remaining night gloom concentrated itself into the solid shapes of Pearl, Redman, Mom Cat with her swaying belly, and one-eyed Paddington. I was filling the food bowls when something light darted along the edges of the yard. It was a pale yellow cat, rangy, its thin tail straight up. It was wary but not wild, and the unconcern of the others showed that it had been there before. But when John and Ginger were leaving yesterday, they had not mentioned a new cat.

It was a neutered male, and over the next few days

he appeared and disappeared regularly both next door and in my own yard. In full sun he was a light orangey gold, like a good cheddar cheese, with narrow orange stripes. He moved always on the edges of things. He would approach, then whirl and trot off, that tail an emblem of courteous retreat. The memory of a collar ringed his neck. When the Willsons returned, the first thing we talked about was this elusive new cat. We asked around and we checked with Animal Control, but our inquiries only confirmed what the ghost of the collar already had told us.

I scowled through the next few days and fought with myself. I knew I should adopt this self-effacing creature. I yearned toward him, but I fled from him, too, from the pain that always seemed to accompany my commitments. Why did I find giving something of myself to a stray cat almost as daunting as giving of myself to my parents? I knew why, really: when the bad things happened to Mother and Dad, I did not give enough to make the bad more endurable. I coped with loss by running away from the reality of it, even from the possibility of it. So, I was afraid of being a care giver even in a situation less complex than the human one. Instead of embracing the responsibility, I fled from it. I squirmed; I was cowardly, and I was selfish.

I was six when Agamemnon kitten died, seven when Pearl Harbor got tangled in my child's head with the Swett Ranch and the Fukuchis. So I had begun to learn then that life was not fair, that loss and sadness were the darker threads of living. They could not be avoided, and by their contrast they made the good moments and the strong times more significant. Not for anything would I have missed Tarik's joyousness, Tai's beauty, nor the insights and questions that Pinky brought me by raising his kittens. I clung to the memories of the bicycle rides with my parents through the wine country. I treasured the fleeting moments that deepened into essences.

I recalled the time in the store with Mother and Dad when I was perhaps thirteen, and needed a pair of "nicer" shoes. The young man brought out a box from which he began with a flourish to remove the tissue. "These are the latest style. Everybody is wearing them."

"That," Dad had replied, "is precisely why we will not buy them."

I recalled also the time, just a few years ago, alone with Mother in the Sun and Moon Restaurant in Concord. She read her fortune cookie, " 'You like Chinese food,' " and we had sputtered like teenagers.

I sighed. The more I embraced life, the more I could give, and receive, and learn. I had known that for such a long time. I was more than half a century old, I gibed at myself; how long did I need to act on my knowledge, to grow into strength?

Mo tipped my scale. The late spring days had cool mornings, and I would look out the kitchen window to see Mo and the slender yellow cat in tentative play on the lawn. If I went outside, Mo would come running, and the new cat would look at me out of big eyes in a small, pointed face. His expression hopeful and polite, he would approach, but if I reached out my hand he skittered away with his long tail aloft. When the breezes blew raw off the straits, Mo shared with him the warm gravel of the driveway, and in the hot afternoons they sought together the shaded bricks of the back terrace.

Then one evening at twilight I found them curled in sleep in the shelter of the blue-flowered agapanthus by the kitchen. Mo had his nose against his friend's neck and one chunky front leg over the narrow golden shoulders. I stood caught in their gentle magic, caught in something atavistic at the backs of their brains and mine. The roots of what I saw — the giving, the accepting — went back somewhere to our shared beginnings before there were either cats or Homo sapiens. Mo in his cat's way had made a promise, an offer, and that was just as plain to me as to the thin stray lying beside him. Watching them pierced me with a strangely deep, aching sadness, and a kind of exultation.

The tightness in my shoulders seeped away. In a few moments the frogs began their evening chorus.

38

SEARCHING

Feathery stickers with razor tips worked through my socks and pricked a scribble of welts onto my ankles. I mopped my face across my arm. My glance carried from the pyracanthas up toward the house through a long, steep sea of tawny foxtails and oats. In the stillness I smelled the parched growth, pungent, like the trails in the long-ago summers of horses.

Up to one side the grasses shuddered and closed behind themselves as if a long snake were flowing down the hill. The motion angled toward me, and there was Mo in a horizontal, stubby-legged line. Over and over he played the notes of a question on the flute of his voice. Behind him, above the grasses, wavered the tip of an orange and yellow tail. I heard a yip much like Priscilla's. I put aside my heavy pruners and gloves to sit on the ground, and

Mo and Cheddar sat with me. With the sun on my arms and tangled in my hair I entered one of those moments of feeling that it was all right to take time for the small, important things.

Cheddar, all angles and thin legs, rolled in a dust bath that pulled him down in an out-of-control slide. He flipped himself like a trout and sprang lightly back up beside me. I ran my hand over his length, and off his springy coat came the dust and the weed heads to leave him as shining as if just groomed. Mo I combed every day, but he looked unkempt and scruffy.

How different they were from each other. The day I had searched for Cheddar through every room and had returned frustrated to the kitchen, he had peered down at me over the ivy from on top of the refrigerator. Mo could never make it even to the drainboard. Last evening out on the lawn Cheddar had leaped to the birch tree and up and over to the roof without breaking his bounding stride. Mo had stumbled to a halt at the base of the tree, and stared up after his friend. I had never seen Mo up in a tree. I could not imagine him on the roof. Cheddar explored its steep gradients as if they were mere continuations of the level ground; at night he appeared at my dormer window two and a half stories above the flagstones. And daily it was he who hunted. Yesterday he had a tiny field mouse that he was batting all across the lawn. When Mo arrived, Cheddar danced over and dropped his mouse in front of him. Mo sniffed it delicately and turned away with an expression that I could read only as, "Yech!" I had never seen him hunt, had never seen him eat anything that was not served in a dish.

I looked at Cheddar now as he pushed his wiry frame against my hand. Only in sleep did his tense lines find slack. Even then, in the way of most cats, his adult sophistication lay over him like silk, the irresistible intent of muscle and claw waiting at the back of his skull. The ego mask of self-awareness, relaxed then but still in place, said that he knew what he was, knew how to play the game. Mo, however, had no more ego mask than a tiny kitten. Asleep or awake he was as vulnerable and as innocent as he looked, a Christmas card mouse gazing in wonder at the heavens. He stole my heart.

Seeing him down here now, with Cheddar and looking as if he felt he lived here, comforted me. This morning he had missed his breakfast again. Night before last he had not come home for dinner or bed for the fourth time in two weeks, and each time he was gone more hours than the last.

But I, too, was away more and more. I had accepted a summer position in Richmond, where I would be teaching a single class of Spanish to teachers four hours a day five days a week, and I felt pressured and anxious. I was the only non-native instructor, and I was facing a classroom full of resentful adults most of whom, until now, had managed to avoid foreign language. For every hour of class I put in more than an hour of intense preparation. I rushed to work, I rushed home. I prepared and ate meals and did house and yard chores through a haze of lesson plans for class and other lesson plans for my private students. The work swept the cats into the uneasy current of my mind, and they swirled almost out of sight. I reached for them in the beginnings and the tired endings of the days, and I always found Cheddar. But Mo was slipping away.

Two mornings later at breakfast I waited for him; I called and searched and called. Finally I hurried off to school with a feeling of impending loss. The next day he was back, slept the night on my bed with his head beside mine on the pillow, then he disappeared again. It was a Thursday, and before Monday morning I had visions of him lying smashed and torn somewhere among the roadside weeds. Wednesday he returned, but when he ate, he kept raising his head from his dish. When I talked to him he seemed only to half hear me.

Mo had something on his mind.

I began putting check marks on the kitchen calendar the days he was not home. July 21 he disappeared again, and the sunny days passed in slow mockery. One evening on the radio I heard part of a news item about two boys who had been trapping cats and torturing them to death to see how much pain they could stand before they died. It was August first. I put the twelfth consecutive check mark on the calendar.

At the end of their term, my Richmond class took me out to a grand lunch, and the remaining summer settled into a less hectic rhythm. I started working out again at the gym, and Earl and I went swimming in Walnut Creek. We went to dinner at Fatapple's. We sat there under a cathedral ceiling of natural wood and exposed pipes and ducts, and looked out at the Albany Hill. And I watched for Mo. I washed his comb and left it ready on the cabinet shelf of the basement hallway.

But three weeks became a month and then a month

and a half. Only Cheddar reached up each morning to
greet me at the door. He was tentative and eager, tightly
coiled in both his body and his mind. His coat was a
chameleon of color and pattern such that I could never
decide whether he had orange stripes that broke into
spots or spots that flowed one into the other. Sometimes
his color seemed flat, but in strong or slanted sun he
caught my breath; he seemed lit from within, lemony air
shimmering through scudding vermilion.

Early September heat withered the lawn. For the third
afternoon temperatures hovered around one hundred.
I took cranberry juice, ice chinking against the blue
Mexican glass, and sat in the pergola under the canopy of
the old buckeye tree. Cheddar trotted out with me, tail
up, polite and apologetic, and lay down on the concrete.
I looked over the valley of evergreen oaks and conifers
to downtown Martinez and the silvery oblong of the old
waterfront cannery. To my nose wafted the decades-
old memory of heavy summer air tart with the smell of
tomatoes cooking there. Beyond, now, across the straits
at the Benicia docks, a tugboat nudged at a ponderous
cargo ship. From its massive side white letters shouted,
"TOYOTA."

Something was pressing on my right shoulder. Turning
I saw Cheddar on his hind legs with his face between the
webbed squares of the chair back. I was as surprised as if
one of the deer that came down from the hills had thrust
its muzzle at me. Like them, he was always lightly poised
on slender limbs. But now he thrust a paw through the
webbing and, in invitation to a game, fished for my arm.
For a few moments we played finger-paw tag, and then

he sat to watch me sip my drink.

After Labor Day my private student load increased again. The weather eased into leaf-spattered gusty breezes and cool nights.

Halloween came and went.

One Saturday afternoon Earl and I were turning out of my driveway and down the hill when he said, "Wait! There's Mo!" He got out and disappeared down into the tall weeds and the loosely graveled steepness of the lane. Shod in dress shoes, I could only sit in the car. The seconds ticked on, and I chewed on my lower lip. I looked at the broken bits of weathered fencing at the top of the lane, and I wished that Earl had not gone down there. For the last three months or so a group of squatters had taken over the derelict stable, and I did not like the looks of the people. Once I had seen two of them wandering zombie-like on the lower road, the young man with black hair hanging in greasy ringlets to his shoulders, and the vacant-eyed girl braless in a loose tank-top.

I glanced at my watch. Five minutes. Here he came.

"Well, maybe it wasn't Mo."

"What made you think it was?" My chest dragged at me.

"The legs. They were white."

Probably Pearl, I thought.

"When I got to the curve, where it gets really steep, my shoe rolled on the gravel, and somebody said, 'Gimme the gun.' " He glanced back down the hill, then looked at me. "I didn't go on down."

Cheddar discovered my bed. Each night he bounded

silently up the stairs — he never thudded, never tripped — to yip away at me before settling down against my feet. Around Thanksgiving he caught a cold, and begged one night to sleep under the covers on my chest. I made a tent of the sheet; in he crawled, ecstatic, and sneezed hugely, wetly, into my face. Great, I thought, groping in the dark for a tissue. Maybe this was carrying chumminess with the cats a bit too far.

Only, it was not "cats" anymore, just "cat." Cheddar sniffled. I drifted back to last February when Mo's respiratory infection had spread first to his intestines and then to one eye. The single detail I could recall vividly was the defeat in those orbs. It was a presence, and I could not push back the fear that he was going to die. It was the same presence that I was seeing in my father's eyes. My father. A strong man, of unconscious dignity, he was reduced by that presence to a wizened plaything of a slow, indecent death, his silvered eyes at bay.

Too much dying, damn it. I had gritted my teeth. I had fed and watered Mo with a dropper, had given him his daily antibiotics, had squeezed the prescription salve into the bloody looking eye. It all had seemed to go on forever, but, as winter softened into spring, he was nearly well again.

It was then that in the cold nights he had burrowed under the covers and stretched his length against me for warmth and companionship. In those moments he was supremely, utterly happy. I would leave the bedside light on to come softly through the top sheet, so that I could peek under and see the liquid expression brimming in his gaze. It took so little, I had thought then, to make his world absolutely perfect for him. The look in his eyes was his profound, unknowing gift to me.

Into the dark now I sighed. That image of Mo's expression was as sharp as if new. But he had been gone so long — four months — that, like Rumer Godden, I was remembering, but I was forgetting — forgetting the exact small things. Which paw, the right or the left front, had had the long toe with the offset claw? Which of my mother's legs had had that perfect beauty mark mole, round and dark and flat, high up on the thigh?

It all receded, receded just as Pinky's body had mingled into the earth, just as Mother's ashes receded among the roots of tall, pink roses. Dulled edges, crumbling and blurring into fine dust, into shadows. Such betrayal. Perhaps it was necessary. Clear images were sharp. The sharpness cut deeply into the soul. Perhaps the diminishing was an inevitable stage of grief, an inescapable path out of an inherent human weakness. Maybe without it we would be paralyzed, pierced with the sharpness of what had been or should have been, unable to move on.

A sudden gust rattled the November rain against the window by my bed. In the dark I felt for Cheddar's head out of the covers; his eyes were closed, and his purring vibrated through my chest. I took a deep breath and willed myself down a slow spiral into sleep.

39

CHRISTMAS

The night had fallen starless and cold. Fog hugged the town, hung among the conifers and among the individual leaves of my oaks, and it wrapped the house in gray wetness. Inside, my kitchen swam in light and warmth. Cheddar lay asleep on his chair. I sat cradling my mug of after-dinner coffee and feeling the tingle of its heat flow up from my fingers and palms into my center.

The last few weeks had hurtled toward the new year: Cheddar's cold had vanished even before he finished the small vial of pink antibiotics; Earl and I had spent Thanksgiving at the nursing home with Dad; classes, students, vacations, and lesson plans had swirled together in a blur. Now, in just four days, it would be Christmas.

Christmas. I should have put up the little artificial tree, I supposed. It looked so real that I always imagined I could smell the pine needles. The white lights and the ornaments — small globes of intense gold, red, silver, and blue — were lovely and festive, and they would commit me to some sort of participation in the season's ritual. There was my problem: Christmas was a family celebration, the only one we had observed at all, and in this house now there was no family. Without that there was no color or gaiety.

I knew with certainty last month that I could not pretend my way through this Christmas. The cooks at the nursing home always prepared a traditional and bountiful Thanksgiving midday dinner, delicious from the crisp, green salad and wine through the moist turkey, yams, mashed potatoes, green beans, tart cranberries, to the pumpkin pies and brownies and coffee. The dining room was spacious, with a wide view to clipped, green lawns and big conifers. Brass chandeliers, startling in their size and brilliance, depended from the ceiling over tables covered in white linen. The carpeted floor muted the voices and the clink of knives and forks.

Normally Dad had to take his meals in his room, usually in bed. But for this big, annual celebration the attendants would dress him and wheel him, already exhausted, down the long hallway. Earl wore a suit and tie, and I my good gray slacks and a tailored silk blouse. Last year I actually had looked forward to it. And it had started so well. I had seen Dad placed in a regular chair. The way he had turned his head and spoken, and his old nervous gesture of rubbing his palms together, created an illusion. I saw my father.

"Hello, Dad!"

"Well, hello. Thank you both for coming." He turned to Earl. "Please, sit down."

But our plates were still more than half full when I had to summon a nurse. She came and wheeled away someone who was not my father at all but just a frail, old man, slumped over, terminally ill and helpless. The wheelchair dragged him away, smaller and smaller, around the corner, where he vanished into the maw of the corridor. I turned away, back to my plate, but I saw only the old man's chalky face and eyes, and the fork slipping from his blue-white hand.

That was last year. This Thanksgiving he had lain in his darkened room with the translucent skin pulling down against the beak of his nose. He ate nothing. He tried to speak, but the hoarsely garbled sounds came only occasionally, in gasping wrenches that I longed to understand.

I ground the heel of my hand against my forehead, and focused on my bright kitchen. My mug was empty and cold. I got up from the table, careful to not wake Cheddar, and tuned the radio to music. As "The Little Drummer Boy" drifted around me, I washed my cup and thought about Christmas Day. Earl and I would open our presents at his apartment, and in the afternoon we would visit Dad. I turned to the back door to take out the evening's garbage, and through the window, like a gentle gift, was an unexpected scene. I turned off my lights, and stepped outside. I stood in the windless dark to look at the house up the slope some two hundred yards beyond the pergola at center stage against the night's curtain. It was a huge house, with wood and glass in about equal amounts. Illumination from a multitude of chandeliers and lamps poured down to hang in the air as gold droplets. Below them the green, yellow, red, and blue points of exterior lights streamed like gauze in the wet scrim of fog. From my radio "Silent Night" floated into the dark. I stood there a long time, and looked, and breathed in the chill and the spicy damp.

Finally, still gazing up the hill, I stepped back, and my leg collided with something furry. "Oops! Sorry." I peered down but saw only a shadowy form gray-black in the black air. "Big Guy? Redman?" No. Too small. "Well, who are ...?" I stooped down just as the cat looked up. Gray face, with a vertical streak of white. White muzzle. White vest and paws. "Mo?" My question echoed in my head. I stared. "Mo!" I stood there stupid with disbelief. But Mo was looking up at me. Wasn't I going to open the door so that he could go in?

It had been five months to the day.

In we went, and Mo checked out Cheddar's empty food bowl. Cheddar, awake now, did not recognize his old friend. He began advancing and making ominous noises, and fluffing up his fur. I ran from one to the other, petting and cajoling them, babbling at them, checking the markings on the gray. I swept up Cheddar, locked him out of the kitchen, and turned back to Mo. This could not be happening. I kept staring. Where had he been? I had forgotten how very square and squat he was anyway, and now he was simply a little tank with whiskers.

I got out his blue dish, wiped it free of dust, poured in a few pellets, and ran to phone Earl.

"Hello?" came his unsuspecting voice.

"Earl," I had to catch my breath, "Earl, Mo is back."

Absolute silence. Then, "Mo is back?"

"Mm-hmm. Just now."

Laughter, incredulous.

By the time Earl and I rang off, Mo was wrapping himself in the little scatter rug in front of the kitchen sink, and the rug was rolling toward the cupboards. I left him again to phone the Willsons.

"John, this is Sandra." A sudden burble of laughter burst from me. "Mo is back!"

Silence. Then, "Mo is back?" Disbelieving laughter. "We're coming right over!"

I rushed around turning on the outside garage light, the porch light, all the living room and dining room lights, and left the front door unlatched. Cheddar was huddled in a corner, confused and frightened. I swooped him up in a quick cuddle. "Mo is back!" I squeaked at him, and kissed the top of his head. He wriggled down and skittered off, and I ran back to the kitchen. Mo's rug lay in a deflated heap. When John and Ginger burst in, Ginger's auburn ringlets bouncing on her neck, Mo was smashing Cheddar's Ping-Pong ball off the walls, off the refrigerator, off the chair legs, off the stove. He was happy, obviously, but also extremely agitated. His play showed an aggressive edge I never had seen before in him, and he would not allow his tail to be touched. Ginger and John and I chatted and laughed over the clatter and thumps of Mo and his ball. He slowed at last, and we all fussed over him and petted him. But when I put my hand under his chest to lift him, he yelled, bit me, and for good measure in a sort of afterthought, hissed. Too much happening too fast.

Much later, when John and Ginger left, I turned off the extraneous lights to sit a while in the living room with Cheddar, whose eyes were stretched wide with the pupils huge and dark. I held him and talked to him as the house settled into a cheerful quiet. At last I left him on the couch in the dark.

In the kitchen Mo, too, was calming down. He sat and washed his face while I opened the door into the bedroom and covered the double bed with an old sheet. Mo watched. He knew what it meant. I turned off all the lights but one, a dim night-light in the bedroom, and closed the door into the hall. In the living room, I sat a while longer with Cheddar, and looked out through the bay window to the downtown Christmas glow muted in the fog. I began to feel sleepy.

"Come on, Cheddar," I yawned. "let's go up to bed."

Holding him, I went for a final peek into the downstairs bedroom. Everything looked gray in the gray light, but finally I saw. There was Mo, a plump, dark mound between the two plumped pillows. His side rose and fell in the rhythm of his contented sleep.

EPILOGUE

The morning after Mo's return I found him still sleeping between those two pillows. After his breakfast he wanted on my lap at the kitchen table, but he was so fat that the short jump turned into a scrambled climb. Once up, he sat there while I finished my oatmeal and looked and looked at him, and asked him how he had acquired such a thick plush of fur.

In two days he and Cheddar were friends again. They began taking daytime naps on the big downstairs bed, and sleeping with me at night upstairs. They spent the rainy winter evenings in boisterous games of tag and tackle all through the living room and dining room, with Cheddar flying above the furniture, and Mo scrambling under or all over it. My little couch will never recover, but by trimming the tufts of pulled threads I have made the damage less noticeable.

Mo still loses me in the house. He calls, that pure sound, a small, lone flute, *Where are you?*

"Here, Mo. Down here, in my office."